the LITTLE BOOK of
CHANGES

the **LITTLE BOOK** *of*

CHANGES

······························

A POCKET I CHING

······························

Peter Crisp

MANDALA
PUBLISHING

San Rafael, California

*This little book
is dedicated to
you.*

CONTENTS

....

I.

INTRO

WHAT *The* **BOOK** IS

It's different!

   The Little Book of Changes is a fresh new interpretation of the *I Ching* (pronounced "yee-jing").

   The *I Ching* is one of the oldest books in the world. It originated in ancient China and has been read and studied by countless numbers of Chinese people for thousands of years. Since 1950, when it was introduced to the Western world in a popular English-language version, it has gained an ever-growing readership around the globe.

I Ching means literally "Book of Changes." It is renowned both as a book of wisdom and as an oracle. (And if you're wondering what an oracle is when it's at home, look at "What Is an Oracle?" on page 158.) In both respects, it is unlike other books: You don't read it from beginning to end, you consult it. In other words, you interact with it. You can engage it in conversation. You can ask it questions.

There are 64 "readings" in *The Book of Changes*. Each one is a meditation on different experiences that occur in the course of our daily lives. As the title suggests, *The Book* is primarily concerned with the changes that life keeps throwing at you and how you respond.

Set against your ever-changing circumstances, *The Book* is there to remind you of the changeless.

Using a simple method that is explained in the next few pages, you will be led to the answers for any questions you may have.

WHY YOU WANT to CONSULT *The BOOK*

It's magical!

For many years, I have been consulting *The Book* on all sorts of questions and in all kinds of situations. It never ceases to amaze me how uncannily accurate and relevant the answers have been. It's as if it somehow knows exactly what is going on with me.

I can't explain it. Eminent psychologist Carl Jung had a go in his introduction to the classic Richard Wilhelm version of the *I Ching*. (If you are interested in knowing more, look at "Introducing the Book to the West" on page 167.) One way you could relate to this spooky phenomenon is that it's like hitting random play on your iPod, or listening to the radio, and the perfect song comes on at just the right moment and it's . . . perfect.

I can tell you that consulting *The Book* is like being able to ask advice from a very powerful, very wise, yet extremely tolerant and easygoing friend or teacher. The better you get to know *The Book*, the more impressive it is.

For example, it will often appear to answer the question behind the question. It's not talking to the superficial personality, the image you present to the world. It addresses the real you, penetrating to the very heart of the matter. Once you have experienced this phenomenon a few times, I think you will agree: There is something magical about this ancient *Book of Changes*—and it still works, even in our skeptical modern world.

WHEN YOU WANT to CONSULT *The BOOK*

It's critical!

It's not called *The Book of Changes* for nothing. When everything is going smoothly and your situation is just as you want it to be, you're not likely to reach for an oracle.

But when you are going through changes—when things are getting rough, stuff is coming at you from left field, right field, from fields you didn't even know existed, when insults turn to injuries, friends appear to let you down, then disappear, only to confirm it, when the proverbial you-know-what hits the fan and you're the fan—this is the time when it can be really helpful and comforting to have a wise, disinterested companion to whom you can turn and say, "Can someone please help me?"

In my experience, these are the times when *The Book of Changes* really comes through, hitting the nail on the head, putting its finger on the cause of the problem, then pointing toward the solution. Yes, for the times that try your soul, a little clarity, a little wisdom, and a little inspiration can go a long, long way.

This is why Confucius recommended that you keep *The Book of Changes* close at hand, because you never know when things are going to change.

HOW to CONSULT *The BOOK*

With respect!

Some of the wisest men ever to walk the earth were involved in *The Book*'s creation, and they held it in the highest regard. (If you want to know more about these men, read "A Brief History of the Book" on page 162.)

So many people for such a long time—we're talking literally billions over millennia—have consulted *The Book*, it has been imbued with a kind of psychic energy. People who are familiar with the *I Ching* claim that reading it is like being in communication with a living person.

The way you approach *The Book* and how you put your question will have a definite influence on the outcome.

All I would add to this excellent advice is this: When you consult *The Book of Changes*, do it with respect.

Respect for *The Book*: Give it a chance to work its magic.

Respect for the question: Trust your own feelings.

Respect for yourself: There's a reason you feel the way you do, and you deserve answers to your questions.

GETTING STARTED

All you need are:
- Three coins (any coins will do)
- Paper and something to write with
- The chart shown on the facing page

Throw the three coins six times. The way the coins fall will give you numbers. The numbers turn into the six lines that make up a *hexagram*, each composed of two three-line *trigrams*. The hexagram is built from the bottom up. (If you want to know more about the trigrams, look at "What's in a Hexagram?" on page 160.) Using the chart, you can find your specific reading.

☯	Heaven ☰	Thunder ☳	Water ☵	Mountain ☶	Earth ☷	Wind ☴	Fire ☲	Lake ☱
Heaven ☰	1	34	5	26	11	9	14	43
Thunder ☳	25	51	3	27	24	42	21	17
Water ☵	6	40	29	4	7	59	64	47
Mountain ☶	33	62	39	52	15	53	56	31
Earth ☷	12	16	8	23	2	20	35	45
Wind ☴	44	32	48	18	46	57	50	28
Fire ☲	13	55	63	22	36	37	30	49
Lake ☱	10	54	60	41	19	61	38	58

LOWER TRIGRAMS

THROWING the COINS

Each side of the coin is associated with a number.

(tails) = **2**   (heads) = **3**

Throw the three coins six times. Each time you throw, look at the coins and add up the numbers.

(tails) (tails) (tails) = **6**   (tails) (heads) (heads) = **8**

(tails) (tails) (heads) = **7**   (heads) (heads) (heads) = **9**

TURNING the NUMBERS into LINES

6 = ▬▬▬▬▬▬▬▬   ▬▬▬▬▬▬▬▬ ☯
                                    CHANGING

7 = ▬▬▬▬▬▬▬▬▬▬▬▬▬▬▬▬
                                    STABLE

8 = ▬▬▬▬▬▬▬▬   ▬▬▬▬▬▬▬▬
                                    STABLE

9 = ▬▬▬▬▬▬▬▬▬▬▬▬▬▬▬▬ ☯
                                    CHANGING

SOME LINES TURN into OPPOSITES

When you throw three tails or three heads, adding up to 6 or 9, you get a *changing line*. Put a symbol, such as an asterisk (here we use a yin-yang sign), next to that line to remind you:

The changing line gives you a little extra information in the first reading and leads you to a second reading. How? By turning that line into its opposite.

MAKING the HEXAGRAMS

Record your lines into a hexagram, **starting at the bottom and working your way up**.

It's not as complicated as it sounds. Perhaps the best way to explain how you can use three coins to answer your questions is to give you an example.

An EXAMPLE

The question I have in mind as I throw the coins is this: "How can I introduce *The Book of Changes* to the modern world?"

I throw the three coins six times. I write my first line at the bottom and work my way up.

6th	(heads) (heads) (heads)	= **9**
5th	(tails) (heads) (heads)	= **8**
4th	(heads) (heads) (heads)	= **9**
3rd	(tails) (heads) (heads)	= **8**
2nd	(tails) (heads) (heads)	= **8**
1st	(tails) (heads) (heads)	= **8**

GETTING MY FIRST READING

So my six-line hexagram, composed of two trigrams, looks like this:

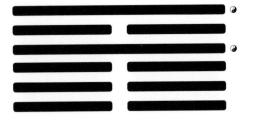

I consult the chart (page 13) for the first reading. The upper trigram is Fire, the lower Earth. This means my first reading is #35, Making Progress.

35
Making Progress

the BOOK

SAYS :: *"The clearer you are, the brighter your light can shine."*

SEES :: you like the rising sun
you are in the ascendancy
taking your place in the sky
this is your chance to shine

SUGGESTS :: the higher the sun rises
the brighter it becomes
as you emerge from obscurity
you shine more and more brightly
enjoy the recognition
only remember your role
as the devoted servant
to a powerful ruler
by practicing your craft
polishing your techniques
to serve your benefactor
your progress is assured

SEE HOW *The* BOOK WORKS

You have to look at it in context. Here am I, the humble scribe, sitting at my desk in Cornwall on a Sunday morning in June, asking the ancient and venerable *Book of Changes* a question.

I put the question just as I am in the midst of the final rewrite of this introduction. Because, dear reader, this is not the first time I've rewritten the introduction. It has been by far the hardest part of *The Book* to write, and the reason it has been so hard is that I have stuck to my initial resolve: to write it ASAP:

As Simply As Possible.

This is a worthy goal, but challenging, as the original *Book* is multilayered and complex.

But here I am on the homestretch of the incredible journey that got me to this point.

So what does *The Book* say in this reading? It resonates on many levels. As ever, it addresses the person behind the question. It says, "The clearer you are, the brighter your light can shine."

It says, "Enjoy the recognition. Only remember your role as the devoted servant to a powerful ruler. By practicing your craft and polishing your techniques to serve your benefactor, your progress is assured."

I feel comforted and reassured by what *The Book* has to say. This is a feeling it frequently, though not always, evokes.

The Book is the powerful ruler and benefactor. In my role as scribe, I am the servant. It is as clear as day.

Again, it's up to me: to practice my craft and polish my techniques so I can do my job to the best of my ability.

So this strikes me as a characteristically wise response. It is also an affirmation of my purpose: to introduce *The Book of Changes* to our modern world in a simple, clear way that is, above all, *accessible*.

But I wonder what those changing lines have to say . . .

WHY I LIKE CHANGING LINES

When consulting *The Book*, I don't try to influence the outcome of the coin-casting ritual. My attitude is this: Don't tell me what I want to hear; tell me how it is. But I do like changing lines.

For one thing, they provide more detail. When the answer is more complete, it demonstrates more vividly the magical properties of *The Book*. The other thing I appreciate about changing lines is that they tend to present the opposite perspective to the main reading.

So, when you get a positive, two-thumbs-up reading, the changing lines often contain warnings. And when you get a negative reading, the changing lines frequently send signals of hope for better times to come.

LET'S LOOK at the CHANGING LINES

All the readings include interpretations of their changing lines. For this one, they are as follows:

4th **9** ████████████████████████████████████

Even if you win the rat race, you'll still be a rat.

6th **9** ████████████████████████████████████

There's no call for aggressive tactics here, unless you are correcting your own mistakes. Being aware of the pitfalls and dangers, and proceeding cautiously, you can certainly achieve your purpose.

WHAT'S the RAT RACE GOT to DO with IT?

"Rat race," according to *The Concise Oxford Dictionary*, means a "fiercely competitive struggle, a struggle to maintain one's position in work or life." This seems to me to be a warning against using *The Book* as a means to an end, as a way to win the rat race, or any other kind of race. And don't make a struggle of it.

I feel reasonably at ease on this score, as my work on this new, accessible version of *The Book* has always been and still is a labor of love. It is not, in any way, shape, or form, intended to compete with any version already out there or still to come. But I welcome the reminder.

WHAT "AGGRESSIVE TACTICS"?

Now, aggression is just about the last thing I'd be guarding against when introducing *The Book of Changes*. But I think I get the point: There's no need for me to be making extravagant claims for *The Book* and hitting you over the head with its significance.

I can also appreciate the suggestion that if I want to be fierce and forceful, I can be that way toward my own writing, especially the editing part. It's not that I have to be ruthless—let's not throw the baby out with the bathwater. But I can be vigilant and rigorous in removing any wording that gets in the way. My guiding principle has always been to let *The Book* speak for itself.

Taking the answer all in all, it is clear: Progress is exactly what I am making as we—the publisher, the editor, and I—hammer out this final draft. At the same time, I must be on my guard against any tendency to be competitive or aggressive. In other words, follow the hip commandment, and be cool.

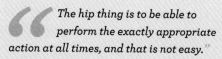

The hip thing is to be able to perform the exactly appropriate action at all times, and that is not easy.

—Geetz Romo, *How To Speak Hip*

GETTING to the SECOND READING

As I throw three heads on my fourth and sixth tosses, I get those two changing lines. So I turn them into their opposites, which results in this pattern:

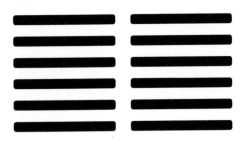

I look at the chart on page 13 to identify my second hexagram. The implication is that by paying heed to the advice in the first reading, it will lead me to the second.

The upper and lower trigrams are both Earth. This means my second reading is #2, Receiving.

2
Receiving

the BOOK

SAYS :: *"It's simple to receive when your heart is full of love."*

SEES :: you like mother earth
the seeds are within you
all you need is light
water and nourishment
with plenty of room to grow
what a harvest it will be

SUGGESTS :: the more you can receive
the more you are able to give
sympathetic souls
kindred spirits
allies and helpers
they are all around you
simply by being open
receptive to the blessings
life has to give
you will prosper and grow

READY to RECEIVE

Well, all I can say after reading my second hexagram, which is indeed the second reading in *The Book*, is yes, please.

COME ON IN, the WATER'S FINE

If you'd like to start consulting right away, go to the chart on page 13. Write down your questions and the answers you get.

> " *Wording your inquiry and writing it down is a necessary part of the process of divination. It will settle your mind into the proper frame of receptivity. In discovering what it is you really wish to know, you learn something of your true feelings.* "
>
> —R. L. WING, *The I Ching Workbook*

REMEMBER

- Write down your question carefully and thoughtfully.

- Throw three coins six times.

- Each throw gives you a number.

- Each number gives you a line.

- You begin at the bottom and build up.

- If you get three heads or three tails, you get a changing line.

- A changing line turns into its opposite and gives you a second reading.

May *The Book* bring you comfort and joy, clarity and wisdom, hope and light.

May this light illuminate your immediate situation so you can see it clearly, because when you *see* with clarity, you know what to *do*. When you know what to *do*, you *feel* good, and when you feel good, you *are* good.

So, with your *Little Book of Changes* in your pocket or purse, you're good to go.

II.

the READINGS

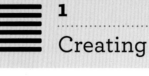

1
Creating

the BOOK

SAYS :: *"It's easy to create when your heart is full of joy."*

SEES :: you like father sky
shedding light on the world
radiating warmth and benevolence
just being who you are
brings good things to life

SUGGESTS :: within you is the power to create
to make things happen
being true to yourself
gives you the courage
you need to be original
believe in yourself
and others will believe in you
whatever you do
DON'T GIVE UP

and the CHANGING LINES ARE ::

9 ██████████████████████████████████████

You've made it. You're flying high. Don't let it go to your head!

9 ██████████████████████████████████████

Water flows to the ocean. Fire reaches for the sun. You have a purpose here, and you have the chance to fulfill it.

9 ██████████████████████████████████████

Your creativity has brought you to a crossroads. You have a choice: Go on blazing a trail of glory, or retreat from the world and work on perfecting your art.

9 ██████████████████████████████████████

Busy. The more successful you are, the more you have to deal with. As your influence grows, there's a danger you will become the victim of your own popularity. By staying in touch with your true feelings, you will remain free from blame.

9 ██████████████████████████████████████

As you enter your chosen field, be open to help from people who are more experienced than you. At the same time, believe in your own ability. If you don't take yourself seriously, who will?

9 ██████████████████████████████████████

Your creative talents remain unrecognized. Don't worry. Your time will come.

2
Receiving

the BOOK

SAYS :: *"It's simple to receive when your heart is full of love."*

SEES :: you like mother earth
the seeds are within you
all you need is light
water and nourishment
with plenty of room to grow
what a harvest it will be

SUGGESTS :: the more you can receive
the more you are able to give
sympathetic souls
kindred spirits
allies and helpers
they are all around you
simply by being open
receptive to the blessings
life has to give
you will prosper and grow

and the CHANGING LINES ARE ::

6 ▬▬▬▬▬▬▬▬▬   ▬▬▬▬▬▬▬▬▬   6th

A power struggle at the top causes harm on both sides. Stay out of it if you can or you might get caught in the crossfire. This is not your fight.

6 ▬▬▬▬▬▬▬▬▬   ▬▬▬▬▬▬▬▬▬   5th

Let your work speak for itself. Don't interrupt.

6 ▬▬▬▬▬▬▬▬▬   ▬▬▬▬▬▬▬▬▬   4th

Keep it to yourself. Whatever you say now will be taken the wrong way. Wait for the controversy to die down before sticking your neck out.

6 ▬▬▬▬▬▬▬▬▬   ▬▬▬▬▬▬▬▬▬   3rd

Don't be too concerned about recognition at this stage. Finish what you start and be satisfied with that.

6 ▬▬▬▬▬▬▬▬▬   ▬▬▬▬▬▬▬▬▬   2nd

You can be your own worst critic. Accept your nature. The thing to remember is that you are unique and original, and this is what you have to offer.

6 ▬▬▬▬▬▬▬▬▬   ▬▬▬▬▬▬▬▬▬   1st

When the first frost of autumn hits, winter is not far behind. Better get ready.

3

Beginning

the BOOK

SAYS :: *"In the beginning is the word*
and the word is now."

SEES :: a new beginning
an exciting development
a storm clearing the air
a new day
when anything is possible

SUGGESTS :: beginning can be a difficult time
when extra care must be taken
whether it's a newborn baby
an idea or an initiative
a journey or a work of art
best to be prepared
when it's time to bring order out of chaos
helping hands are most welcome
once the clutter has been cleared
the dust has settled
the scene is set
let us begin

and the CHANGING LINES ARE ::

TOSS

6

6th

Fate seems to be conspiring against you. You've got to know when to walk away (and know when to run!).

9

5th

Just because you're paranoid doesn't mean they're not out to get you. When you don't have the confidence of others, proceed with extreme caution.

6

4th

When you're in a fix, don't be too proud to accept help. The right helper at the right time can get you out of trouble and put you back on the road.

6

3rd

If you enter uncharted territory without a guide or a map, you're looking for trouble.

6

2nd

Bide your time. Things appear to be falling apart. Whom can you trust? On what can you depend? You.

9

1st

Obstacles, difficulties, hindrances. Pause for thought. What you need is an intelligent approach to intelligence.

4

Playing the Fool

the BOOK

SAYS :: *"If you lack experience, you need a good teacher. If you have a good teacher, pay attention and do what the teacher tells you."*

SEES :: you like a mountain stream
full of rushing enthusiasm
the exuberance of young life
a fool on the brink

SUGGESTS :: the folly of youth
is a fact of life
playing the fool
goes with the territory
but there comes a time
when you have to grow up
if you listen to what is being said
you can receive the gift of wisdom
and not be fooled again

and the CHANGING LINES ARE ::

9 ████████████████████

What do you do with someone who won't listen, who just goes on playing the fool? Temper justice with mercy. Punishment is meant to improve the behavior, not make it worse.

6 ██████████████ ██████████████

Stay in touch with the innate wisdom of the young. Approach life with the heart of a child.

6 ██████████████ ██████████████

Are you deluded by your own projections? Are you about to make a fool of yourself again? *The Book* suggests: don't.

6 ██████████████ ██████████████

Are you wasting your time on an adolescent fantasy? Is it really worth it?

9 ████████████████████

Remember when you were young and foolish? A little tolerance goes a long way. A little kindness never hurt anyone.

6 ██████████████ ██████████████

There comes a time when you have to grow up and start taking the business of life more seriously. A little self-discipline is needed. Life is not a game.

5

Waiting

the BOOK

SAYS :: *"Patience is a gift. Like kindness, you have an abundant reserve of patience within you. Learn how to use it and you'll see a beautiful transformation in your life."*

SEES :: you like clouds in a blue sky
pretty as a picture
a sunny interval
a pause for reflection

SUGGESTS :: waiting is an art
ancient and timeless
waiting is a seed
full of life's certainty
waiting is a drop
on its way to becoming a river
waiting is knowing
timing is everything
while you're waiting
eat, drink, and be merry
for tomorrow we dine

and the CHANGING LINES ARE ::

6 ▬▬▬▬▬▬▬▬▬   ▬▬▬▬▬▬▬▬▬

Are you in the pits? Have all your efforts been in vain?
Sometimes help comes from unexpected quarters. A happy
outcome can appear in a form that, at first, seems strange.

9 ▬▬▬▬▬▬▬▬▬▬▬▬▬▬▬▬▬▬

Take time out to enjoy the simple pleasures life can afford.
You deserve it.

6 ▬▬▬▬▬▬▬▬▬   ▬▬▬▬▬▬▬▬▬

Wait. This is a dangerous situation. Remain calm. Stand fast.
Be brave.

9 ▬▬▬▬▬▬▬▬▬▬▬▬▬▬▬▬▬▬

Stuck in the mud? Spinning your wheels will just get you in
deeper. Once you appreciate the gravity of your situation,
you discover a way out.

9 ▬▬▬▬▬▬▬▬▬▬▬▬▬▬▬▬▬▬

Draw a line in the sand. Across this line, they do not pass.

9 ▬▬▬▬▬▬▬▬▬▬▬▬▬▬▬▬▬▬

Waiting on the meadows. Sweet! Enjoy it while it lasts.

6
Resolving Conflict

the BOOK

SAYS :: *"When you can find peace within yourself, you will find peace all around you."*

SEES :: you like the inner diplomat
observing the conflict
discovering hidden agendas
digging into the causes
of the dangers and difficulties

SUGGESTS :: take a deep breath
a big step back
resolving inner conflicts
enables you to find solutions
to external problems
sometimes doing nothing
is better than doing the wrong thing
once you make peace with yourself
you can make peace with anyone

and the CHANGING LINES ARE ::

9 ▬▬▬▬▬▬▬▬▬▬▬▬▬▬▬▬▬▬

When you engage in an unjust conflict, even if you win, you will lose in the end. A hollow victory will bring you under attack again and again.

9 ▬▬▬▬▬▬▬▬▬▬▬▬▬▬▬▬▬▬

If you are in the right and the authorities are on your side, the conflict can be resolved to your satisfaction.

9 ▬▬▬▬▬▬▬▬▬▬▬▬▬▬▬▬▬▬

You're so caught up in the conflict, you are not seeing clearly. Accept your situation. There's not a lot you can do about it at this point. What you can affect is your attitude. Be at peace with yourself, no matter what.

6 ▬▬▬▬▬▬▬▬   ▬▬▬▬▬▬▬▬

In times of danger, dig deep. Draw on your inner strength. Don't focus on the rewards—just get the job done.

9 ▬▬▬▬▬▬▬▬▬▬▬▬▬▬▬▬▬▬

When you know you can't win, retreat. Timely withdrawal implies no blame. If you can see it coming, avoid the calamity.

6 ▬▬▬▬▬▬▬▬   ▬▬▬▬▬▬▬▬

By not reacting to the attacks on you, you defuse the conflict. Don't worry—it will work out in the end.

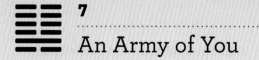

7
An Army of You

the BOOK

SAYS :: *"You are a force to be reckoned with. Discipline is the key to success."*

SEES :: you as a natural leader
with the support of people
who have good reason
to come out and fight for you
when the cause is just
and the need is great

SUGGESTS :: you have courage and strength
the ability to inspire others
but just as muscles need exercise
if they are to be strong
your talents must be employed
for you to develop and grow
when the leader lacks discipline
what hope is there for the army?

and the CHANGING LINES ARE ::

6 ▇▇▇▇▇▇▇▇▇▇   ▇▇▇▇▇▇▇▇▇▇   6th

The campaign is complete. Victory is yours. Share the rewards with the people who helped you achieve them.

6 ▇▇▇▇▇▇▇▇▇▇   ▇▇▇▇▇▇▇▇▇▇   5th

The game is afoot. Now's the time to act! May your progress be swift and your aim be true.

6 ▇▇▇▇▇▇▇▇▇▇   ▇▇▇▇▇▇▇▇▇▇   4th

When you're up against a vastly superior force, there's no shame in a well-ordered retreat.

6 ▇▇▇▇▇▇▇▇▇▇   ▇▇▇▇▇▇▇▇▇▇   3rd

You have to get rid of the dead wood if you want the tree to be healthy and grow.

9 ▇▇▇▇▇▇▇▇▇▇▇▇▇▇▇▇▇▇▇▇▇▇▇▇▇▇▇▇   2nd

A good leader spends time on the ground sharing experiences with the people doing the work: recognition, reward, reinforcement.

6 ▇▇▇▇▇▇▇▇▇▇   ▇▇▇▇▇▇▇▇▇▇   1st

In the beginning of a campaign, good organization is essential.

8

Joining Forces

the **BOOK**

    SAYS :: *"You are the river and the river is you."*

    SEES :: you are like a drop of water
joining together
with other drops of water
to form one mighty river

    SUGGESTS :: now is the time to unite
with kindred spirits
in a common cause
working together
you can achieve great things
that you cannot do alone
for you to take the lead of such forces
to be the center of attention
you will need to be strong
consistent and clear
(so if you're still not sure
ask the oracle once more)

and the CHANGING LINES ARE ::

6 ▬▬▬▬▬▬   ▬▬▬▬▬▬

6th

Make sure you get it right from the start. If the beginning is all wrong, what hope is there for the outcome?

9 ▬▬▬▬▬▬▬▬▬▬▬▬▬

5th

Fair play is the foundation of good teamwork. A unity based on trust and conviction is always stronger than one fraught with fear and suspicion.

6 ▬▬▬▬▬   ▬▬▬▬▬

4th

When you find a good person or group of people that you trust and believe in, show your loyalty. Let them know how you feel.

6 ▬▬▬▬▬   ▬▬▬▬▬

3rd

You're hanging out with the wrong people. Not only are they holding you back, they're keeping you from the right people.

6 ▬▬▬▬▬   ▬▬▬▬▬

2nd

If you are happy to be a follower and feel genuine respect for the leader, trust your feeling. If you're just going along for the ride, watch out.

6 ▬▬▬▬▬   ▬▬▬▬▬

1st

Content is everything. If you are sincere, you will be blessed with good fortune.

9

Gently Does It

the BOOK

SAYS :: *"Like a gentle breeze on a hot summer's day, your influence is subtle yet most welcome."*

SEES :: you like a beautiful day
gentle breezes are blowing
exquisite clouds adorn
a brilliant blue sky

SUGGESTS :: the gentle art of persuasion
in the eyes of others
you are what you appear to be
invest the time and effort
both in your appearance
and how you express yourself
only remember
clouds are not merely ornamental
they serve a vital purpose:
the delivery of rain

and the CHANGING LINES ARE ::

9

With the downpour comes relief. Through your patient efforts, you have finally attained your goal. Take extra care or you might snatch defeat from the jaws of victory.

9

Sincerity coupled with loyalty is a winning combination. By serving the mutual interests of both parties, everyone's a winner.

6

Being gentle in your handling of the situation is not a sign of weakness. Your strength is in holding on to what you know to be true. Then you need not fear.

9

You blew it again! If only you'd held back and bided your time. If married or in a partnership, a row is almost inevitable.

9

The way ahead is blocked. Bide your time. Consider an alternative route.

9

Do what suits you. Find the place where you feel comfortable. How can you go wrong with that?

10
Treading Carefully

the BOOK

SAYS :: *"There's no doubt you're going places now, but watch your step and don't get ahead of yourself."*

SEES :: you finding your way in the world
where your position is defined
both by your inner character
and how it is outwardly expressed

SUGGESTS :: it's not what you do
it's the way that you do it
tread carefully
you are working with powerful forces
that can take you where you want to go
so show some respect
but don't lose your sense of humor
a respectful attitude
combined with
a cheerful expression
will win you friends
in both high and low places

and the CHANGING LINES ARE ::

9 ▬▬▬▬▬▬▬▬▬▬▬▬▬▬▬▬▬▬▬▬▬▬▬▬   6th

Look at what you've done. If you've done well, enjoy your rewards. Let's celebrate.

9 ▬▬▬▬▬▬▬▬▬▬▬▬▬▬▬▬▬▬▬▬▬▬▬▬   5th

When you embark on a bold course of action, you are taking your chances. However, if you are aware of the dangers and how to deal with them, your adventure can be a great success.

9 ▬▬▬▬▬▬▬▬▬▬▬▬▬▬▬▬▬▬▬▬▬▬▬▬   4th

You're riding a tiger, so be extremely cautious. The danger is real, but by being extra careful, you can avoid being hurt.

6 ▬▬▬▬▬▬▬▬   ▬▬▬▬▬▬▬▬   3rd

Be careful. If you tread on a tiger's tail, he just might turn around and bite you.

9 ▬▬▬▬▬▬▬▬▬▬▬▬▬▬▬▬▬▬▬▬▬▬▬▬   2nd

Stay on the path. You walk your walk and are not affected by the opinions of others. You are happy with your own company.

9 ▬▬▬▬▬▬▬▬▬▬▬▬▬▬▬▬▬▬▬▬▬▬▬▬   1st

Keep it simple. Be happy with your rate of progress. Your restless mind with its endless ambitions will only make you miserable. Ignore it if you can.

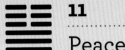

11
Peace

the BOOK

SAYS :: *"You discover your heaven on earth when you find true peace within yourself."*

SEES :: you like a peaceable domain
enjoying and appreciating
the benign influence of your heaven
the receptive nature of your earth
the symmetry of your seasons
the elegance of your day
the comfort of your night

SUGGESTS :: be at peace with yourself
this is your heaven on earth
rain brings the seed to life
sunlight enables it to grow
working with nature
you achieve a bountiful harvest
as the well-being within you rises
sickness will simply disappear

and the CHANGING LINES ARE ::

TOSS

6 ▬▬▬▬▬▬ ▬▬▬▬▬▬ 6th

Your outer defenses are crumbling. Accept your fate. With-draw into the inner circle, composed of the people you know you can trust. Guard yourself in silence.

6 ▬▬▬▬▬▬ ▬▬▬▬▬▬ 5th

With the generosity of your nature, you bring all different kinds of people together and a good time is had by all.

6 ▬▬▬▬▬▬ ▬▬▬▬▬▬ 4th

A shower of blessings, a time of harmony—rich and poor get together like good neighbors and friends. Sweet.

9 ▬▬▬▬▬▬▬▬▬▬▬▬▬ 3rd

Everything changes; it's always the same. Persevere in times of difficulty. *The Book* suggests: less complaining, more sustaining.

9 ▬▬▬▬▬▬▬▬▬▬▬▬▬ 2nd

Prosperous times will attract all kinds of people to your en-terprise. Trusting those who are close to you allows you to pay more attention to those who are far away.

9 ▬▬▬▬▬▬▬▬▬▬▬▬▬ 1st

In times of peace and prosperity, your ability to achieve your goals is enhanced. It's only natural that like-minded people are drawn to help you.

12
Standing Still

the BOOK

SAYS :: *"When all around you are losing their heads, you can keep yours— simply by standing still."*

SEES :: you like a wise leader
withdrawing from the fray
when all is discordant and confusing
when chaos is the order of the day
you stand for dignity
your position is clear

SUGGESTS :: stand still
very very still
take a good look around
bide your time
mind your own business
don't be fooled
by tempting offers
until you know it's time
to make your move
then go for it
if you stand still for too long
it may turn to stagnation

and the CHANGING LINES ARE ::

9 ██████████████████████████████

6th

The time for standing still is over. A good thing, too. You didn't know how much more standing still you could stand.

9 ██████████████████████████████

5th

Time to stop standing still and spring into action. Ask yourself: What if it should fail? But don't let that stop you. Have a plan B.

9 ██████████████████████████████

4th

It's your call. Look for the mutual benefits to all parties concerned and you'll make the right decision.

6 ████████████   ████████████

3rd

Once you acknowledge your mistakes you can begin to put them right.

6 ████████████   ████████████

2nd

Stick to your principles and everything will turn out right in the end. Have patience.

6 ████████████   ████████████

1st

In a time of standstill, be true to yourself. When things start moving again, you will be in a good position to succeed.

13

The Fellowship

the **BOOK**

SAYS :: *"At the heart of any fellowship worthy of the name is a great love that is shared by your fellows."*

SEES :: you like a good fellow
entertaining friends
serving the cause
following your heart

SUGGESTS :: the foundation of your fellowship
is the common cause
binding you together
with clarity on the inside
strength on the outside
great things are possible
but you will need clear leadership
good organization
if you want to succeed

and the CHANGING LINES ARE ::

9 ▬▬▬▬▬▬▬▬▬▬▬▬▬▬▬▬▬▬▬▬▬

The common meadows belong to the people. Friends meet in the open air. It is a wonderful, easygoing fellowship.

9 ▬▬▬▬▬▬▬▬▬▬▬▬▬▬▬▬▬▬▬▬▬

When the fellowship has been kept apart by circumstances, great joy attends the reunion.

9 ▬▬▬▬▬▬▬▬▬▬▬▬▬▬▬▬▬▬▬▬▬

It takes two to tango. Stay out of the fight. Seek reconciliation.

9 ▬▬▬▬▬▬▬▬▬▬▬▬▬▬▬▬▬▬▬▬▬

Hostile or divisive forces have infiltrated your fellowship. Suspicion breeds suspicion, paranoia feeds on itself. The longer it goes on, the worse it gets.

6 ▬▬▬▬▬▬▬▬▬   ▬▬▬▬▬▬▬▬

When the fellowship is fragmented and people are driven by selfish motives, you are heading for disaster. Be aware of this potential and try to stop it before it happens.

9 ▬▬▬▬▬▬▬▬▬▬▬▬▬▬▬▬▬▬▬▬▬

In the beginning of a communal enterprise, openness is the key. Transparency inspires trust.

14
Heavenly Treasure

the BOOK

SAYS :: *"A treasure shared is a treasure doubled."*

SEES :: you like the sun
high in the sky
shining brightly
to light up your world
revealing both the good and the bad

SUGGESTS :: in the light of this new day
take a good look at your life
get rid of the evil
nurture the good
dig the riches you discover
share them with the world
express yourself clearly
stay in control
you will be richly rewarded
when you find your treasure on earth
it feels like heaven

and the CHANGING LINES ARE ::

9 ▬▬▬▬▬▬▬▬▬▬▬▬▬▬▬▬▬▬▬▬▬ 6th

You are blessed by good fortune. Your devotion is rewarded from above, your sincerity is recognized by one and all.

6 ▬▬▬▬▬▬▬▬▬   ▬▬▬▬▬▬▬▬ 5th

You've reached an exalted position. Be accessible but retain your dignity. This is your time of good fortune. Enjoy it.

9 ▬▬▬▬▬▬▬▬▬▬▬▬▬▬▬▬▬▬▬▬▬ 4th

Don't envy those who are better off, nor look down on those who are worse. Be happy with a little, be content with your lot.

9 ▬▬▬▬▬▬▬▬▬▬▬▬▬▬▬▬▬▬▬▬▬ 3rd

Don't keep it to yourself. Such a heavenly treasure is for the benefit of everyone.

9 ▬▬▬▬▬▬▬▬▬▬▬▬▬▬▬▬▬▬▬▬▬ 2nd

You've found the treasure. Now you must use the appropriate vehicle to convey it to where it can do the most good. Reliable people are worth their weight in gold.

9 ▬▬▬▬▬▬▬▬▬▬▬▬▬▬▬▬▬▬▬▬▬ 1st

When things start to go your way, don't let it go to your head. There are still difficulties to be overcome.

15

Modesty Becomes You

the BOOK

SAYS :: *"Being as humble as you can be (without disappearing) you shine with an inner light."*

SEES :: you like a hidden mountain
composed and self-contained
empty of conceit
full of genuine affection
making you radiant

SUGGESTS :: modesty suits you
reduce your excesses
clear what needs clearing
build what needs building
edit what you do not need
polish what you want to keep
such refinements will bring success

and the CHANGING LINES ARE ::

6 ▬▬▬▬▬▬▬▬ ▬▬▬▬▬▬▬▬

6th

When modesty finds its full expression, it creates order. It's a discipline that allows you to transcend ego and achieve true and lasting benefits for you and your world.

6 ▬▬▬▬▬▬▬▬ ▬▬▬▬▬▬▬▬

5th

Modesty can be mistaken for weakness, but don't be tempted into boasting of your strength. Nobody likes a show-off.

6 ▬▬▬▬▬▬▬▬ ▬▬▬▬▬▬▬▬

4th

Modesty is not something to hide behind. Recognition of your ability and commitment enables you to accomplish more.

9 ▬▬▬▬▬▬▬▬▬▬▬▬▬▬▬▬▬▬▬▬

3rd

Your natural modesty is the key to your success. When the rewards and recognition come, follow the hip commandment: Be cool.

6 ▬▬▬▬▬▬▬▬ ▬▬▬▬▬▬▬▬

2nd

Being modest does not mean keeping quiet. Express your actual feelings if you want to have a real influence.

6 ▬▬▬▬▬▬▬▬ ▬▬▬▬▬▬▬▬

1st

Make no promises you cannot keep. When you're facing a new challenge, you need all your concentration to get the job done.

16

Enthusing

the BOOK

SAYS :: *"To be enthused is to be filled with divine inspiration. When you are inspired, you are inspiring."*

SEES :: you like a summer storm
your enthusiasm resounding
far and wide
like rolling thunder
like heavenly music

SUGGESTS :: as a thunderstorm relieves tension
refreshing the earth
music brings joy to the heart
following the line of least resistance
you get the people moving
they are on your side
like a rainbow bridge
you make the connection
between heaven and earth
you've got the whole world
in your hands
when you know the secret of enthusiasm

and the CHANGING LINES ARE ::

6 ▬▬▬▬▬▬   ▬▬▬▬▬▬

There's a big gap between expectation and reality here. Awakening from a false enthusiasm can only be a good thing.

6 ▬▬▬▬▬▬   ▬▬▬▬▬▬

Frustration. Obstacles. Stress. It's enough to make you ill, and it frequently does. Try not to react. Don't let it get under your skin.

9 ▬▬▬▬▬▬▬▬▬▬▬▬▬▬▬

No doubt about it. You retain friends and supporters, who are attracted by your enthusiasm. Together, you can achieve great things.

6 ▬▬▬▬▬▬   ▬▬▬▬▬▬

Don't let those above you dim your enthusiasm. You who hesitate are lost.

6 ▬▬▬▬▬▬   ▬▬▬▬▬▬

You know straightaway what the real deal is here. Secure in this knowledge, you can relax. Your take on the situation is right on.

6 ▬▬▬▬▬▬   ▬▬▬▬▬▬

You may feel the need to show off and make an impression. Like you have to boast a bit. You don't.

17
Following

the BOOK

SAYS :: *"Following the path that feels right to you will take you where you really want to go."*

SEES :: a storm on the water
joy in motion
a natural sequence of events
a fabulous footpath

SUGGESTS :: the path you are on was made for you
if you stay on it
you will find it easy going
when you learn to listen
you will be heard
when you learn to follow
you will know how to lead
your ability to adapt
to the changes around you
inspires confidence in your followers
when you have had a long day on the trail
better get some rest

and the CHANGING LINES ARE ::

6 ▬▬▬▬▬▬▬▬ ▬▬▬▬▬▬▬▬

You achieve recognition. You advance along your chosen path. Enjoy your rewards—you deserve them.

9 ▬▬▬▬▬▬▬▬▬▬▬▬▬▬▬▬▬▬▬

Recognizing and following the path that leads you to your promised land—this is your great good fortune.

9 ▬▬▬▬▬▬▬▬▬▬▬▬▬▬▬▬▬▬▬

Follow through and you will fulfill your ambition. Go your own way—just as you are. Sincerity will bring clarity. Clarity will show the way.

6 ▬▬▬▬▬▬▬▬ ▬▬▬▬▬▬▬▬

When you connect with the right people who enable you to follow your true path, it often means parting company from the ones who were leading you astray.

6 ▬▬▬▬▬▬▬▬ ▬▬▬▬▬▬▬▬

The company you keep can seriously affect how well you perform. Beware the weak and seek out the strong, for they will bring out the best in you.

9 ▬▬▬▬▬▬▬▬▬▬▬▬▬▬▬▬▬▬▬

Exciting events are unfolding. If you want to be part of the action, get out more.

18

Working On It

the BOOK

SAYS :: *"When you know the job has got to be done, the sooner you get to work, the better you will begin to feel."*

SEES :: you in a state of inertia
somehow stuck in a moment
like stagnant water
something in you
needs to be moved
wants to be moving

SUGGESTS :: the longer you leave it
the worse it gets
the garden that needs weeding
the mess that needs clearing up
the heart that needs to be understood
get weeding—get clearing
seek understanding
and you will find fulfillment
when you bring order out of chaos
you show the way
for others who may be stuck

and the CHANGING LINES ARE ::

TOSS

9 ▬▬▬▬▬▬▬▬▬▬▬▬▬▬▬

What does all work and no play make you? Take a break and have some fun.

6th

6 ▬▬▬▬▬▬   ▬▬▬▬▬▬

Job done. You've cleared up the mess and put things back in order. You deserve a break.

5th

6 ▬▬▬▬▬▬   ▬▬▬▬▬▬

Once the rot sets in, it becomes harder and harder to get rid of it. The sooner you start, the better.

4th

9 ▬▬▬▬▬▬▬▬▬▬▬▬▬▬▬

Sometimes when you're clearing up, you have to get your hands dirty. Wear rubber gloves if you like—just get cleaning. You will feel so much better when it's done.

3rd

9 ▬▬▬▬▬▬▬▬▬▬▬▬▬▬▬

The mess you've inherited was not created deliberately. It's much more satisfying to clean it up than to worry about who's to blame.

2nd

6 ▬▬▬▬▬▬   ▬▬▬▬▬▬

The mess may not be of your making. It may be a legacy mess. However, it's now your responsibility to clear it up. Just do it.

1st

19
....
Approaching Greatness

the **BOOK**

SAYS :: *"How do you approach greatness?*
Very humbly."

SEES :: you like a good teacher
whose clarity and enthusiasm
make the subject easy to approach
the lake is deep
the earth spreads far and wide

SUGGESTS :: it's all in your approach
a humble heart and a tolerant attitude
create a safe atmosphere
where people want to do their best
this is how a good teacher
becomes a great teacher
once you get the ball rolling
maintain the momentum
the excitement in the early stages
is bound to diminish
defeat the threat of boredom
by keeping your approach fresh

and the CHANGING LINES ARE ::

TOSS

6 ▓▓▓▓▓▓▓▓▓▓▓▓   ▓▓▓▓▓▓▓▓▓▓▓▓   6th

Great is the good fortune of the student who can approach a true teacher with a humble heart.

6 ▓▓▓▓▓▓▓▓▓▓▓▓   ▓▓▓▓▓▓▓▓▓▓▓▓   5th

A wise leader attracts capable people and encourages them to use their abilities to the full.

6 ▓▓▓▓▓▓▓▓▓▓▓▓   ▓▓▓▓▓▓▓▓▓▓▓▓   4th

Be open-minded. You have gathered able people around you who can make good things happen. Let them.

6 ▓▓▓▓▓▓▓▓▓▓▓▓   ▓▓▓▓▓▓▓▓▓▓▓▓   3rd

Things are going well. But complacency can undo your good work. If it's already happened, apologize and move on.

9 ▓▓▓▓▓▓▓▓▓▓▓▓▓▓▓▓▓▓▓▓▓▓▓▓▓▓▓   2nd

When a collaboration works, your burden is lightened. A joint approach leads to progress.

9 ▓▓▓▓▓▓▓▓▓▓▓▓▓▓▓▓▓▓▓▓▓▓▓▓▓▓▓   1st

Doors are opening. Things are looking up. You approach greatness by standing up for what you know to be right.

20

Taking a Long Look

the BOOK

SAYS :: *"By finding a high place, you gain the perspective you need."*

SEES :: you like seeing and being seen
the wind blows where it will
you move among the people
observing their ways

SUGGESTS :: a period of contemplation
a place of elevation
so you can see the big picture
looking at your life
what you have to offer the world
the intensity of your focus
the sincerity of your devotion
combine to give you a power of seeing
that enables you to have a profound effect
on the attitudes of people
without them even knowing how it happens

and the CHANGING LINES ARE ::

9 ████████████████████████████████   6th

Contemplate life itself. Life within you and without you.

9 ████████████████████████████████   5th

Contemplate this: How are you affecting the people around you? Now, consider what's going on inside you to cause these effects. Change begins within you.

6 ████████████████   ████████████   4th

Good people invite you into their world. Enjoy the hospitality they offer and express your gratitude.

6 ████████████████   ████████████   3rd

Look at what you are contemplating. Honestly. Do you really want to go there?

6 ████████████████   ████████████   2nd

Life as seen through a crack in the door—you need to get out more.

6 ████████████████   ████████████   1st

Childlike imaginings are all very well if you're just having fun at home. But if you want to be taken seriously in the real world, you'd better start acting like a grown-up.

21
Biting Through

the BOOK

SAYS :: *"Energetic and decisive action is required to remove the obstacle blocking your progress."*

SEES :: an electrical storm
great flashes of lightning
illuminating the scene
so you can see clearly

SUGGESTS :: when an obstacle needs to be removed
a problem must be solved
you've got to lay down the law
act swiftly
like an animal in the wild
biting through the umbilical cord
of its newborn offspring
you have to cut through
whatever's getting in the way
of your natural progress
with whatever is available to you

and the CHANGING LINES ARE ::

TOSS

9 ▬▬▬▬▬▬▬▬▬▬▬▬▬▬▬▬▬▬▬▬▬▬▬ 6th

When people are deaf to all warnings and keep making the same mistakes, you need to do something dramatic to focus their attention.

6 ▬▬▬▬▬▬▬▬▬   ▬▬▬▬▬▬▬▬▬ 5th

You're aware of the dangers but you know you're right to proceed. Be fair in your demands and you will receive satisfaction.

9 ▬▬▬▬▬▬▬▬▬▬▬▬▬▬▬▬▬▬▬▬▬▬▬ 4th

Because of your determination to take on the opposition and remove the obstacles, you'll be under attack. You'd best be well protected.

6 ▬▬▬▬▬▬▬▬▬   ▬▬▬▬▬▬▬▬▬ 3rd

You're stirring up some old grudges here. It's a painful procedure but a necessary one. It will be good to get through these things.

6 ▬▬▬▬▬▬▬▬▬   ▬▬▬▬▬▬▬▬▬ 2nd

The case is easy to settle and you meet with little resistance. No blame.

9 ▬▬▬▬▬▬▬▬▬▬▬▬▬▬▬▬▬▬▬▬▬▬▬ 1st

Your authority is threatened. You hope a warning shot may be enough. But be prepared to take more drastic action.

22
Grace

the BOOK

SAYS :: *"The world is a beautiful place*
when your life is full of grace."

SEES :: you like a fire in the mountain
a radiant inner glow
brightening and gladdening
every aspect of your existence

SUGGESTS :: as the moon reflects
the glory of the sun
you too can create
beautiful reflections
to enrich your world
attend to the details
refine and polish the threads
you weave together
to create a tapestry of delight
so you can live
in a state of grace

and the CHANGING LINES ARE ::

9 ▮▬▬▬▬▬▬▬▬▬▬▬▬▬▬▬▮   6th

No unnecessary ornamentation is required. Form serves function. The design does not get in the way; it brings out the value of the content.

6 ▮▬▬▬▬▬▮   ▮▬▬▬▬▬▮   5th

You find grace in your surroundings: a walk in the hills, relaxing in nature. Who needs material riches when you can enjoy such simple pleasures?

6 ▮▬▬▬▬▬▮   ▮▬▬▬▬▬▮   4th

Like a winged horse, you rise above your situation. You can go on pushing the boundaries or return to a simpler style. The choice is yours.

9 ▮▬▬▬▬▬▬▬▬▬▬▬▬▬▬▬▮   3rd

Are you leading a charmed existence? Don't get too comfortable or you might lose your edge. Without your edge, life would be so dull.

6 ▮▬▬▬▬▬▮   ▮▬▬▬▬▬▮   2nd

If you want to get ahead in the world, good grooming is essential. Why do you think they say someone is being groomed for success?

9 ▮▬▬▬▬▬▬▬▬▬▬▬▬▬▬▬▮   1st

It is more graceful to go on foot than to ride in the carriage under a false pretext.

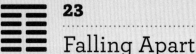

23

Falling Apart

the BOOK

SAYS :: *"When the old order is collapsing, find shelter in the sanctuary of your heart. Prepare to embrace the new."*

SEES :: you like a crumbling mountain
a house on the verge of collapse
the old order passing away
the new order rising

SUGGESTS :: keep a low profile
conserve your energy
there's not much you can do now
when things fall apart
it's time to let them go
stay true to your generous nature
don't let the bad times
put a dent in your benevolence
hold on to your inner equilibrium
stay safe in a quiet heart
until the good times return

and the CHANGING LINES ARE ::

TOSS

9

6th

The worst of your fall from grace is over. Evil has eaten itself. Now you can start again. The core of your being is intact and ready to put forth fresh growth.

6

5th

When things are falling apart, you find out who your true friends are. Lay down your arms and surrender to their tender loving care. You could use some right now.

6

4th

Something's wrong when you can't sleep at night. Try to figure out what it is and put it right. If you can't manage on your own, get help.

6

3rd

Enough is enough. You can only take so much. A clean break is indicated.

6

2nd

Feeling isolated? Under attack? Consider your options. Sometimes just changing your position can alleviate the pain.

6

1st

Is your authority being undermined? Has your reputation been tarnished by hearsay? Don't be too concerned. You know what you're doing.

the READINGS   **73**

24
....
The Point of Return

the BOOK

SAYS :: *"When you come to a major turning point, just for a moment, your whole world stands still."*

SEES :: you like coming home
returning to the light
celebrating your life
in the company of good friends

SUGGESTS :: let nature take its course
just as the earth
in the depths of winter
at the time of the solstice
stops for a moment
before turning
making its journey back toward the sun
you too have arrived at a place
where you can begin the journey
back to where you belong
it's a cause for celebration

and the CHANGING LINES ARE ::

6 ▮▮▮▮▮▮▮▮▮▮   ▮▮▮▮▮▮▮▮▮▮

If you keep missing the point and straying from where you truly belong, you are going to get hurt. Only a change of heart can save you now.

6 ▮▮▮▮▮▮▮▮▮▮   ▮▮▮▮▮▮▮▮▮▮

You're big enough to admit your mistakes and return to the way. Your heart is in the right place, and it shows.

6 ▮▮▮▮▮▮▮▮▮▮   ▮▮▮▮▮▮▮▮▮▮

Don't follow the herd. Do your own thing, even if it means doing it alone.

6 ▮▮▮▮▮▮▮▮▮▮   ▮▮▮▮▮▮▮▮▮▮

Do you keep changing your mind? Going back on your decisions? Too many changes are not good for you.

6 ▮▮▮▮▮▮▮▮▮▮   ▮▮▮▮▮▮▮▮▮▮

Come home to where you belong. You'll be in good company—even when you are alone.

9 ▮▮▮▮▮▮▮▮▮▮▮▮▮▮▮▮▮▮▮▮▮▮▮▮

It's OK to stray from the path as long as you get back on it.

25

Innocence

the BOOK

SAYS :: *"Your fundamental nature has not
changed. It is as innocent as the
day you were born. If you lose touch
with this inner sense, what will
become of you?"*

SEES :: you like a benign ruler
grounded in your true nature
full of virtue
overflowing with kindness

SUGGESTS :: being true to yourself
you can't go wrong
expecting the unexpected
you're not taken by surprise
being attuned to the times
following your better instincts
you bring good things to life
life brings good things to you

Mk 10:13 — / Mat 18:2 — / Mat 19:14 — / Luke 18:15 —
Become like a child to enter the Kingdom.
✷ Care of the inner child.

and the CHANGING LINES ARE ::

9 ▮▮▮▮▮▮▮▮▮▮▮▮▮▮▮▮▮▮▮▮▮▮▮▮▮

Hang on. The time may not be right. Is it instinct or impulse? Best to be sure.

9 ▮▮▮▮▮▮▮▮▮▮▮▮▮▮▮▮▮▮▮▮▮▮▮▮▮

Whatever's troubling you will pass. If it's not your fault, why take the blame? If you're not really sick, why pay for medicine?

9 ▮▮▮▮▮▮▮▮▮▮▮▮▮▮▮▮▮▮▮▮▮▮▮▮▮

Do your own thing. Give it your all—you've got nothing to lose and everything to gain.

6 ▮▮▮▮▮▮▮▮▮▮▮▮   ▮▮▮▮▮▮▮▮▮▮▮

Accidents will happen. Good people have bad luck. That's just how it is.

6 ▮▮▮▮▮▮▮▮▮▮▮▮   ▮▮▮▮▮▮▮▮▮▮▮

Focus on what you're doing. Enjoy the simple pleasure of getting the job done.

9 ▮▮▮▮▮▮▮▮▮▮▮▮▮▮▮▮▮▮▮▮▮▮▮▮▮

Follow your heart. It knows you better than you know yourself.

26

Holding On to Greatness

the BOOK

SAYS :: *"You can draw on the ancient wisdom
teachings to strengthen your character."*

SEES :: heaven in the mountain
hidden treasures revealed
the wisdom of the past
made available to you today

SUGGESTS :: your success is so close
you can taste it
all this energy building up inside
is about to be released
get ready for the ride of your life
hold on
hold fast to what you know to be true
hold back till the time is just right
hold on to your dreams
as they turn into reality

and the CHANGING LINES ARE ::

TOSS

9 ━━━━━━━━━━━━━━━━━━━━━━━━━━━━━ 6th

A stairway to heaven. The success you have been seeking is yours for the taking.

6 ━━━━━━━━━━━━ ━━━━━━━━━━━━ 5th

By not overreacting, you diminish the power of dissension. By remaining calm you can diffuse the tension that agitated people tend to create.

6 ━━━━━━━━━━━━ ━━━━━━━━━━━━ 4th

Anticipate trouble before it happens. Stop it before it starts.

9 ━━━━━━━━━━━━━━━━━━━━━━━━━━━━━ 3rd

Lead by following. Keep your ear close to the ground. Be alert to any sign of danger.

9 ━━━━━━━━━━━━━━━━━━━━━━━━━━━━━ 2nd

Your progress is temporarily halted—like someone took the wheels off! You need to repair your vehicle, or you won't get too far.

9 ━━━━━━━━━━━━━━━━━━━━━━━━━━━━━ 1st

Greatness comes in its own time—you can't force it. Hold on to the power stored within you and hold back till the time is right.

27

Nourishing

the BOOK

SAYS :: *"Watch your mouth."*

SEES :: you like cultivating character
both physical and spiritual
tranquility is the key
to your growth and well-being

SUGGESTS :: the food and drink you consume
will determine the health you enjoy
the things you express
the words you choose to say them
will define your state of mind
just as delicious nourishing food
sustains the body
expressions that are beautiful and true
nurture the spirit
the nourishment you provide for yourself
can also nourish those around you

and the CHANGING LINES ARE ::

9 ▮▮▮▮▮▮▮▮▮▮▮▮▮▮▮▮▮▮▮▮▮▮▮   6th

Well-nourished, both physically and spiritually, you can now face the dangers and overcome the difficulties.

6 ▮▮▮▮▮▮▮▮▮▮   ▮▮▮▮▮▮▮▮▮▮   5th

Going into unfamiliar territory, you're likely to need help. If you're not sure of the outcome, don't invest too heavily.

6 ▮▮▮▮▮▮▮▮▮▮   ▮▮▮▮▮▮▮▮▮▮   4th

You're hungry like a tiger, your appetite for success driving you onward and upward.

6 ▮▮▮▮▮▮▮▮▮▮   ▮▮▮▮▮▮▮▮▮▮   3rd

Sensual gratification and the pursuit of pleasure will be your undoing. You've got to know when to quit.

6 ▮▮▮▮▮▮▮▮▮▮   ▮▮▮▮▮▮▮▮▮▮   2nd

Your natural state is to support yourself. If you are dependent on someone else for your support, you will never be truly comfortable.

9 ▮▮▮▮▮▮▮▮▮▮▮▮▮▮▮▮▮▮▮▮▮▮▮   1st

There is magic, working wonders in your life. Don't lose it by looking at what works for other people and wondering if you should be like them.

28

Taking a Load Off

the BOOK

SAYS :: *"Find a way to lighten your load before something gives."*

SEES :: you like a beam that is sagging
an overloaded structure
on the edge of collapse
a system that is being pushed
to its limit

SUGGESTS :: if you've taken on too much
you have two choices
lighten the load
by discarding some items
or get help carrying it
when the burden becomes insupportable
something's got to give
and it's likely to be you
only by identifying the real problem
can you discover a lasting solution

and the CHANGING LINES ARE ::

6 █████████████████   █████████████████

You're in over your head. Some things in life are worth your sacrifice. But is this one of them?

9 ███████████████████████████████████████

Have you seen new growth on an old tree? Where there's life, there's always hope.

9 ███████████████████████████████████████

You've got the extra support just when you need it. Don't abuse it, or you'll lose it.

9 ███████████████████████████████████████

Overload. If you refuse to listen to good counsel and go on carrying a burden you are not really able to bear, your collapse is almost inevitable.

9 ███████████████████████████████████████

When you're not overloaded and you are content with your lot, extraordinary things can happen. Like new growth on an old tree, you can experience the vitality of youth all over again.

6 █████████████████   █████████████████

Careful. When moving a heavy, valuable object, take extra care, especially when setting it down.

29

Making Good Your Escape

the BOOK

SAYS :: *"You're in a tight spot. By remaining calm and true to your nature, you'll get out of this place."*

SEES :: you in a deep ravine
but just as water
remains true to its nature
finding its own level
flowing ever onward
you can still reach your goal

SUGGESTS :: even when things appear
to be abysmal
and you are at your lowest ebb
keep the faith
remain true to your principles
maintain your integrity
the consistency you show
when surrounded by danger
is an inspiration
to those who follow

and the CHANGING LINES ARE ::

6 ▬▬▬▬▬▬▬ ▬▬▬▬▬▬▬

You're in a tight spot, all right! Bound and gagged, imprisoned. There's no escape from this situation. All you can do is hang tough and ride the time.

9 ▬▬▬▬▬▬▬▬▬▬▬▬▬▬▬

You're in serious trouble but not in over your head. Not yet, anyway. Get out of there while your head's still above water.

6 ▬▬▬▬▬▬▬ ▬▬▬▬▬▬▬

A jug of wine? A bowl of rice? Given the circumstances, it's a veritable feast.

6 ▬▬▬▬▬▬▬ ▬▬▬▬▬▬▬

Hang in there. Whichever way you go will get you into trouble. Do nothing till the dangers have passed and the situation has improved.

9 ▬▬▬▬▬▬▬▬▬▬▬▬▬▬▬

It's a disaster. Until conditions improve, don't try to accomplish too much. Just get through this.

6 ▬▬▬▬▬▬▬ ▬▬▬▬▬▬▬

You've fallen into a pit. Bad luck. You are going to need help getting out of it.

30

Your Latest Flame

the BOOK

SAYS :: *"You're on fire. You light up your world
with the intensity of your enthusiasm
and the clarity of your vision."*

SEES :: you like a roaring fire
fueled by your passion
flames of love are dancing
spreading warmth and light all around

SUGGESTS :: trees and grass cling to the earth
sun and moon cling to the sky
flames cling to the wood
you cling to the light within
that enables you to shine
return to the source again and again
so you don't burn yourself out
agreeing to agree
accepting your position in life
you are clearly where you are meant to be
keeping the home fires burning

and the CHANGING LINES ARE ::

9 ━━━━━━━━━━━━━━━━━━━━━━━━━━━

6th

Don't be too hard on yourself, but do try and root out some of your bad habits. If something is seriously wrong, look for the causes of the symptoms. If you can eradicate evil, the good will prevail.

6 ━━━━━━━━━━━━   ━━━━━━━━━━━

5th

Sometimes it's good to cry, to release the flood of tears. Acknowledging your grief, a natural process of healing begins.

9 ━━━━━━━━━━━━━━━━━━━━━━━━━━━

4th

A fire made of straw will blaze up brilliantly but soon burns itself out. A meteor is a thrilling sight but quickly forgotten.

9 ━━━━━━━━━━━━━━━━━━━━━━━━━━━

3rd

At the end of the day there's a temptation to indulge in drunken revelry or wallow in melancholy. Resist it.

6 ━━━━━━━━━━━━   ━━━━━━━━━━━

2nd

Blazing with the light of the midday sun, you radiate feelings of benevolence and good fortune. The flowering of your creative self-expression is at its height.

9 ━━━━━━━━━━━━━━━━━━━━━━━━━━━

1st

Another new day and the world is kicking into life. Your mind is all over the place. Intent on your purpose, you compose yourself so you can acquire the clarity you need to get the job done.

31

The Woo Factor

the BOOK

SAYS :: *"When you want to win people over to your point of view, you don't necessarily need to wow them, but you do have to woo them."*

SEES :: you like a lake on a hill
a reservoir of received wisdom
you say: come on in
the water's fine

SUGGESTS :: there are people you naturally like
and naturally they like you
such affinities work well together
to increase your sphere of influence
respect is the foundation
for any long-lasting relationship
whether it is with your audience
your friend or your spouse
show some respect in the house

and the CHANGING LINES ARE ::

6 ▇▇▇▇▇▇▇▇▇▇ ▇▇▇▇▇▇▇▇▇▇

6th

Empty words persuade no one. When your words are meaningful and backed up by genuine passion, people will be influenced by them.

9 ▇▇▇▇▇▇▇▇▇▇▇▇▇▇▇▇▇▇▇▇▇▇▇

5th

If you overexert your influence, you run the risk of a pain in the neck. Having one and/or being one.

9 ▇▇▇▇▇▇▇▇▇▇▇▇▇▇▇▇▇▇▇▇▇▇▇

4th

If your thoughts are flitting here and there, your influence on people and events is negligible. Focus your mind, listen to your heart, and the cause for remorse will disappear.

9 ▇▇▇▇▇▇▇▇▇▇▇▇▇▇▇▇▇▇▇▇▇▇▇

3rd

The attraction here is distinctly below the belt. If you follow your desire and not your heart, you're heading for trouble—again. When will you ever learn?

6 ▇▇▇▇▇▇▇▇▇▇ ▇▇▇▇▇▇▇▇▇▇

2nd

The influence you're under is not coming from your heart. Therefore, it's not in your control. You'd be wise to wait until it is.

6 ▇▇▇▇▇▇▇▇▇▇ ▇▇▇▇▇▇▇▇▇▇

1st

Your influence is barely felt. It may just be a whim or a passing fancy. Either way, it's no big thing.

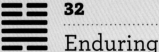

32

Enduring

the BOOK

SAYS :: *"You are self-contained, relying on your inner resources—you stand firm. You abide."*

SEES :: you like a force of nature
thunder rolling
high wind blowing
a reed bending with the breeze
a flower turning toward the sun
forever changing yet always the same

SUGGESTS :: seasons wax and wane
according to fixed laws
everything comes and goes
in its proper time and place
all around you: change
there may be a storm outside
but inwardly you are calm
the enduring present belongs to you

and the CHANGING LINES ARE ::

6 ▬▬▬▬▬▬▬ ▬▬▬▬▬▬▬

If you're always in a hurry, looking anxiously ahead, constantly changing your mind, no good can come of it. Calm down.

6 ▬▬▬▬▬▬▬ ▬▬▬▬▬▬▬

Whether you uphold tradition or make a break from it depends on your own good judgment. Keep an open mind and adapt to the situation. Be flexible without being *too* flexible.

9 ▬▬▬▬▬▬▬▬▬▬▬▬▬

No game is afoot. You're looking for love in all the wrong places.

9 ▬▬▬▬▬▬▬▬▬▬▬▬▬

Don't let the ups and downs get to you. Don't lose the inner quality on which you depend. Get back in touch—with yourself.

9 ▬▬▬▬▬▬▬▬▬▬▬▬▬

Through your actions, the remorse you've been feeling disappears. What a relief.

6 ▬▬▬▬▬▬▬ ▬▬▬▬▬▬▬

If you want to compress something, you must first let it fully expand. If you want to make something that will last, take your time.

33

Retreating

the BOOK

SAYS :: *"Sometimes, a retreat into a place
of tranquility is just what the doctor
ordered."*

SEES :: you like a distant mountain peak
keeping the demons at bay
you are not angry
you are reserved

SUGGESTS :: retreat need not be running away
it can be a sign of strength
by putting distance between yourself
and the hostile forces on the attack
you bring them to a standstill
you remain calm and dignified
because even when retreating
especially when retreating
a human being must have dignity

and the CHANGING LINES ARE ::

TOSS

9

6th

No doubt about it—you are free to go. Liberating yourself from a losing battle fills you with good cheer. The clarity you consequently feel reveals the path you must follow.

9

5th

Yes, you are withdrawing from the scene, but you can still be friendly.

9

4th

When it is appropriate, a well-organized retreat can only help you and your cause. At the same time, it may well defuse hostile forces.

9

3rd

When a retreat is blocked or halted, it's a stressful and dangerous time. Keep your people close—the ones you trust.

6

2nd

You may not be winning this battle, but even when you have to withdraw, you never lose sight of your long-term goal: winning the war.

6

1st

The tail end of a retreat is a dangerous place to be. Don't try anything till you're in a safer place.

34

Coming from
a Powerful Place

the BOOK

SAYS :: *"A righteous combination of power and goodness makes you irresistible. Use it, don't abuse it."*

SEES :: you like a quiet storm
generating excitement
clearing the air
inspiring enthusiasm

SUGGESTS :: you know the feeling
it's the right time
the right place
the right people
you have got it made
still you must be careful
how you proceed
only going through appropriate channels
remember where you're coming from
and you can see where you want to go:
a place of harmony and goodwill
where love is the order of the day

and the CHANGING LINES ARE ::

6 ▆▆▆▆▆▆▆▆▆▆   ▆▆▆▆▆▆▆▆▆▆

A goat is butting a hedge and its horns are entangled. It can't go forward and it can't go back. The only way out of this predicament is to stop struggling. Calm down and gently disentangle yourself.

6 ▆▆▆▆▆▆▆▆▆▆   ▆▆▆▆▆▆▆▆▆▆

The gates to success are open. All you have to do now is walk through them. Release the tension. Drop the shoulders. Take a deep breath . . .

9 ▆▆▆▆▆▆▆▆▆▆▆▆▆▆▆▆▆▆▆▆▆▆▆

The obstacles give way, the gates open—the only question now: Are you ready to make your entrance?

9 ▆▆▆▆▆▆▆▆▆▆▆▆▆▆▆▆▆▆▆▆▆▆▆

A frustrated goat butts a hedge and its horns become entangled. Careful!

9 ▆▆▆▆▆▆▆▆▆▆▆▆▆▆▆▆▆▆▆▆▆▆▆

The gates to success are beginning to open. Be excited but not too excited.

9 ▆▆▆▆▆▆▆▆▆▆▆▆▆▆▆▆▆▆▆▆▆▆▆

You may feel the power, but are you really in a position to exercise it? If not, better wait until you are.

35

Making Progress

the BOOK

SAYS :: *"The clearer you are, the brighter your light can shine."*

SEES :: you like the rising sun
you are in the ascendancy
taking your place in the sky
this is your chance to shine

SUGGESTS :: the higher the sun rises
the brighter it becomes
as you emerge from obscurity
you shine more and more brightly
enjoy the recognition
only remember your role
as the devoted servant
to a powerful ruler
by practicing your craft
polishing your techniques
to serve your benefactor
your progress is assured

and the CHANGING LINES ARE ::

9 ▬▬▬▬▬▬▬▬▬▬▬▬▬▬▬▬ 6th

There's no call for aggressive tactics here, unless you are correcting your own mistakes. Being aware of the pitfalls and dangers, and proceeding cautiously, you can certainly achieve your purpose.

6 ▬▬▬▬▬▬▬ ▬▬▬▬▬▬▬ 5th

It's all going your way. Don't be too concerned about gains and losses. You'll come out ahead, whatever happens. Enjoy your progress.

9 ▬▬▬▬▬▬▬▬▬▬▬▬▬▬▬▬ 4th

Even if you win the rat race, you'll still be a rat.

6 ▬▬▬▬▬▬▬ ▬▬▬▬▬▬▬ 3rd

The progress you make is the direct result of the support you receive from allies and helpers. This is not to be denied; it is to be acknowledged and celebrated.

6 ▬▬▬▬▬▬▬ ▬▬▬▬▬▬▬ 2nd

Your progress is checked, but only temporarily. In the end, you'll be as happy with the outcome as if your mother had wished it for you.

6 ▬▬▬▬▬▬▬ ▬▬▬▬▬▬▬ 1st

If others appear to doubt you, remain confident and calm. If they are rude, don't let it get to you. Simply let your light shine.

36

Darkness Descending

the BOOK

SAYS :: *"While the forces of darkness surround you, keep a low profile and stay safe at home."*

SEES :: the sun setting on you
darkness spreading over the earth
lanterns glowing in your sanctuary
your little world is full of light

SUGGESTS :: your talent may not be recognized
your true worth may not be valued
you let many things pass
but you are not fooled
keep the flame burning
keep it safe
the darker it gets out there
the brighter it looks inside

and the CHANGING LINES ARE ::

6 ▬▬▬▬▬▬▬   ▬▬▬▬▬▬▬

6th

Don't despair. The darkness will feed on itself until there is nothing left. The light of a new day will inevitably shine again.

6 ▬▬▬▬▬▬▬   ▬▬▬▬▬▬▬

5th

It's wrong and you know it's wrong, but they've got the upper hand for now. Exposing them is too dangerous. Keep it to yourself.

6 ▬▬▬▬▬▬▬   ▬▬▬▬▬▬▬

4th

You can see the coming storm. So you are able to weather it or, if necessary, get out of its way.

9 ▬▬▬▬▬▬▬▬▬▬▬▬▬▬▬

3rd

Accidents happen. Sometimes they work to your advantage, but don't let that lull you into a false sense of security. The danger is not over yet.

6 ▬▬▬▬▬▬▬   ▬▬▬▬▬▬▬

2nd

Is it your feelings that are hurt, or are you really wounded? If you can still help others even though you're hurting yourself, do it. What goes around comes around.

9 ▬▬▬▬▬▬▬▬▬▬▬▬▬▬▬

1st

Hard times. You could be really stretched. You might have to go without. People may try to put you down. Don't let them.

37
Family Affair

the BOOK

SAYS :: *"Thank God for the people who embrace and support you through thick and thin."*

SEES :: you like a blazing fire
radiating good cheer
filling the house with warmth
making it feel like home

SUGGESTS :: home is where the hearth is
to keep the fire dancing
feed the flame
give it room to breathe
gather 'round the familiar fire
with your tribe
where you know you belong
partaking of your good food
drinking your good health
giving thanks
for your refuge from the world

and the CHANGING LINES ARE ::

9 ▬▬▬▬▬▬▬▬▬▬▬▬▬▬▬▬▬

Work rules (especially if you work at home). The breadwinners of the family must be given the time and space they need to do their jobs well.

9 ▬▬▬▬▬▬▬▬▬▬▬▬▬▬▬▬▬

There's no need for fear in a family ruled by love.

6 ▬▬▬▬▬▬▬   ▬▬▬▬▬▬▬

How fortunate is the family where a good woman is happy at home. If you have such a treasure, you will want to protect it.

9 ▬▬▬▬▬▬▬▬▬▬▬▬▬▬▬▬▬

Family rows—we all have them. Try not to overreact or be too severe. At the same time, a total lack of discipline will end in tears. Find the happy medium.

6 ▬▬▬▬▬▬▬   ▬▬▬▬▬▬▬

Nurture the family and provide healthy nourishment. What's good for them is also good for you.

9 ▬▬▬▬▬▬▬▬▬▬▬▬▬▬▬▬▬

Domestic harmony depends on order. When you establish clear boundaries from the outset, you can avoid most of the rows. If everything is vague and undefined, look out!

38
....
The Strange Attraction
of Opposites

the BOOK

SAYS :: *"Our differences can be a cause of
conflict or the elements of a dance.
When opposites unite in harmony,
what a joy."*

SEES :: a flame on the lake
dancing on the surface of the water
beautiful and strange

SUGGESTS :: opposing viewpoints
different ways of seeing
walking contradictions
such fascination you hold for some people
and they have a hold over you
while it is true opposites attract
no matter how much you are attracted
how deeply you get involved
retain your individuality
at all costs
give each other space
the flame must stay above the water
or it will be extinguished

and the CHANGING LINES ARE ::

9 ████████████████████████████████

6th

No one falls out harder than "best friends." We've all been there. In the end, if you can remember the beginning of the friendship, you will want to be reconciled.

6 ████████████   ████████████

5th

Strange days have found you. When a friend is prepared to put up with all this for your sake, you have a friend indeed.

9 ████████████████████████████████

4th

Feeling isolated? At odds with the world? Out in the cold? At times like these, one good friend can make all the difference. Two good friends—even better!

6 ████████████   ████████████

3rd

All too often it seems as though circumstances and people are conspiring against you. You're checked, hindered, and insulted. Yes, it's annoying and frustrating, but don't let it get to you. Persist. It will turn out well in the end.

9 ████████████████████████████████

2nd

Serendipity at work. A chance encounter leads to resolution of a misunderstanding.

9 ████████████████████████████████

1st

A change for the better. Instead of chasing the object of your desire, let it come to you.

39

Overcoming Difficulties

the BOOK

SAYS :: *"Adversity is a teacher, and the
difficulties you face are the lessons to
be learned. At times like this, you can
use all the help you can get."*

SEES :: water on the mountain
a difficult situation
dangers all around
obstacles dead ahead

SUGGESTS :: greet difficulty with respect
as you would a teacher
who demands your ingenuity
sharpens your focus
strengthens your resolve
enjoy the process of discovering
solutions to the problems
accept the help of friends
persevere
deep in your heart you know
you will overcome

and the **CHANGING LINES ARE** ::

TOSS

6 ████████████ ████████████   6th

It may not be your problem, and you're entitled to walk away. But you have the experience and the know-how to solve it. Working with good people to put things right is indeed satisfying.

9 ████████████████████████████   5th

Isn't it amazing that when you most need them, friends have a way of showing up or getting in touch?

6 ████████████ ████████████   4th

Don't take on more than you can handle. If you have friends and allies, now is the time to call on them. Together, you can overcome the obstacles.

9 ████████████████████████████   3rd

Sometimes the obstacles are insurmountable, the dangers more than you can safely handle. At such a time, there's no disgrace in turning back. Your people will be glad if you do.

6 ████████████ ████████████   2nd

It's not your fault that so many obstacles have arisen, but it is your duty to remove them. Just do it.

6 ████████████ ████████████   1st

When confronted by an obstacle, stop and consider. What's the easiest way to remove it? There's always an easy way.

40

Delivering

the BOOK

SAYS :: *"What a relief! Like a thundercloud, pregnant with pent-up moisture, you can now release your cargo of rain."*

SEES :: you like a downpour of rain
a sweet summer storm
clearing the air
relieving the tension

SUGGESTS :: the time for agonizing is over
whether it's a package or a promise
a project or an invitation
it's time to deliver
when it comes to delivering judgments
temper justice with mercy
don't dwell on mistakes
forgive failings
as thunder fades away
as the rain washes all clean

and the CHANGING LINES ARE ::

6 ▬▬▬▬▬▬ ▬▬▬▬▬▬   6th

Your bow is strong. Your arrow is straight and its point is sharp. The target is clear. If you have put in the practice, how can you miss?

6 ▬▬▬▬▬▬ ▬▬▬▬▬▬   5th

Deliver yourself. When people realize you are in earnest, that you are undeniable, they will yield.

9 ▬▬▬▬▬▬▬▬▬▬▬▬▬   4th

When great deeds are called for, you need good people you can depend on. Passengers and hangers-on just get in the way. Lose the losers and win the day.

6 ▬▬▬▬▬▬ ▬▬▬▬▬▬   3rd

Enjoying your success? Tempted to flaunt your recently acquired wealth? Don't set yourself up for others to rip you off.

9 ▬▬▬▬▬▬▬▬▬▬▬▬▬   2nd

Your aim is true. You deserve the recognition, so savor the rewards.

6 ▬▬▬▬▬▬ ▬▬▬▬▬▬   1st

Well done—you've delivered. It's a success. Take a moment to enjoy the peace and quiet, the calm after the storm.

41

Decreasing

the BOOK

SAYS :: *"Hard times can bring out the best in you. With fewer distractions on the outside, you can discover the wealth within."*

SEES :: a lake in the foothills
a cool still place
ideal for reflection

SUGGESTS :: less is more
when times are hard
resources are low
going without on the outside
can motivate you to go within
where your true riches
are waiting to be discovered
at the same time
a decrease in negativity
is a definite plus

and the CHANGING LINES ARE ::

9 ▬▬▬▬▬▬▬▬▬▬▬▬▬▬▬▬▬▬▬▬

Your work is rewarded with good fortune. Now you can afford help, but maybe you simply prefer working alone.

6 ▬▬▬▬▬▬▬▬ ▬▬▬▬▬▬▬▬

All the signs are favorable. You're in luck.

6 ▬▬▬▬▬▬▬▬ ▬▬▬▬▬▬▬▬

Sort yourself out. If you make a sincere effort to overcome bad habits, you'll be amazed how people will support you.

6 ▬▬▬▬▬▬▬▬ ▬▬▬▬▬▬▬▬

Two's company, three's a crowd.

9 ▬▬▬▬▬▬▬▬▬▬▬▬▬▬▬▬▬▬▬▬

If you can be of service, good. But don't waste your valuable time helping people who don't appreciate it.

9 ▬▬▬▬▬▬▬▬▬▬▬▬▬▬▬▬▬▬▬▬

You are ahead of schedule. You can take off early, or you can help others. The choice is yours.

42

Increasing

the BOOK

SAYS :: *"What an opportunity! You have a real chance to improve your lot in life. Seize the moment while you can."*

SEES :: wind and thunder
movement and change
a season of growth
a time for new developments

SUGGESTS :: increasing your influence in the world
may require a change of character
where you see people doing good
emulate them
where you can recognize your own faults
work on getting rid of them
do something for the community
and they will do something for you
this time of increase will not last
so make the most of it

and the CHANGING LINES ARE ::

9 ████████████████████████████████   6th

When you keep your good fortune to yourself, you invite trouble. By enriching others, you enrich yourself.

9 ████████████████████████████████   5th

If your heart is in the right place, you don't need to make a fuss. This is your good fortune: Your sincerity will be recognized.

6 ██████████████   ██████████████   4th

Keep to the middle path. Don't be swayed by extremes. Make sure that any increase in power or wealth is distributed fairly.

6 ██████████████   ██████████████   3rd

Even accidents seem to help your cause. Be sincere and you'll come to no harm. Your influence is recognized at the highest levels.

6 ██████████████   ██████████████   2nd

Someone up there really does love you. You are attracting all kinds of positive energy into your life, making you virtually unstoppable. Use this increase for the benefit of one and all, then your lucky streak can go on and on.

9 ████████████████████████████████   1st

The help you receive from above puts you in a position to achieve great things—things you've always wanted to do. Lucky.

43

Breaking Through

the BOOK

SAYS :: *"Fortune favors the brave. This is the breakthrough you've been waiting for and working toward."*

SEES :: a heavenly lake
a gathering of forces
an accumulation of energies
ready to explode

SUGGESTS :: when people have been holding you back
and circumstances conspiring against you
you can turn it around
through bold and decisive action
break through
once you've made it to the other side
share the rewards with your supporters
keep the momentum going
only remember
making a breakthrough
will expose you to new dangers
so keep your eyes open

and the CHANGING LINES ARE ::

6 ▬▬▬▬▬▬▬▬▬ ▬▬▬▬▬▬▬▬▬

You've made it: your breakthrough. This is when complacency can set in and undo all your good work. Don't let it.

9 ▬▬▬▬▬▬▬▬▬▬▬▬▬▬▬▬▬▬▬▬▬

Time for some serious weeding in the garden. If you just pull off the tops, those weeds will come right back. Eradicate them and the plants you love will have room to grow.

9 ▬▬▬▬▬▬▬▬▬▬▬▬▬▬▬▬▬▬▬▬▬

Are you in such a rush to attain your goal that you ignore the obvious pitfalls? Stubbornly charging ahead is going to backfire on you. But if you refuse to listen, what's the use of good advice?

9 ▬▬▬▬▬▬▬▬▬▬▬▬▬▬▬▬▬▬▬▬▬

After the breakthrough, people may turn against you. They may find you guilty by association when you are in fact innocent. Make no mistake: You have the resolve and the strength to walk through the storm and emerge unscathed.

9 ▬▬▬▬▬▬▬▬▬▬▬▬▬▬▬▬▬▬▬▬▬

You get a wake-up call: Are you ready for this? Have you prepared? Guard yourself against the dangers and don't be afraid.

9 ▬▬▬▬▬▬▬▬▬▬▬▬▬▬▬▬▬▬▬▬▬

These are big steps you are about to take. Are you sure you're up to it? If not, you could take a fall.

44

Coming Together

the BOOK

SAYS :: *"Meeting people halfway, so both parties benefit, is a good thing. But be aware of people who might try to take advantage."*

SEES :: you like the winds of heaven
celestial influences
inspire you to communicate
your vision to the people

SUGGESTS :: when the benign influence of heaven
meets the receptive earth
all creatures prosper
when people are drawn together
to make the world a better place
transparency is key
any hidden agenda will bring harm
be prepared to compromise
but come to the meeting
with a clear vision
of what you are trying to achieve
watch out for weaker elements
who appear harmless
yet could undermine all your good work

and the CHANGING LINES ARE ::

9 ▬▬▬▬▬▬▬▬▬▬▬▬▬▬▬▬▬▬▬▬▬▬▬

If you've had enough and want to enjoy some peace and quiet, just ask everybody to go away and leave you alone. You're entitled.

9 ▬▬▬▬▬▬▬▬▬▬▬▬▬▬▬▬▬▬▬▬▬▬▬

The confidence you have in yourself inspires confidence in others. In turn, the confidence you have in them is rewarded with their enthusiastic cooperation.

9 ▬▬▬▬▬▬▬▬▬▬▬▬▬▬▬▬▬▬▬▬▬▬▬

You can't afford to alienate anyone at this stage. You never know who is going to turn out to be an ally just when you need one.

9 ▬▬▬▬▬▬▬▬▬▬▬▬▬▬▬▬▬▬▬▬▬▬▬

Some days, even the simplest steps are tricky. Be mindful of the dangers and proceed with caution.

9 ▬▬▬▬▬▬▬▬▬▬▬▬▬▬▬▬▬▬▬▬▬▬▬

You have detected a negative influence at work. You can control the damage by containing it.

6 ▬▬▬▬▬▬▬▬▬▬   ▬▬▬▬▬▬▬▬▬▬

When you detect that a negative person is trying to undermine the meeting, immediately check it. Even the young and inexperienced with little power or responsibility can cause major damage if left to run wild. Nip it in the bud.

45

Gathering

the BOOK

SAYS :: *"Whether it's a festival or a ceremony, a concert or a congress, a collaboration or a movement, getting together with like-minded individuals renews your sense of purpose—and it's fun!"*

SEES :: you drawn to a gathering
of people like you
united by a common cause
inspired by a shared vision

SUGGESTS :: bring something to the table
offering your talents
with sincerity
will bring success
as your influence grows
you may encounter resistance
watch out for slings and arrows
hold on to the shield of hope
wear the armor of patience
sharpen your sword of truth
put on a good show

and the CHANGING LINES ARE ::

6 ███████████████   ███████████████

When people try to get together, misunderstandings all too often get in the way. So don't be afraid to express your true feelings. A little honesty goes a long way.

9 ████████████████████████████████████

You have your rightful place in this gathering and your reasons for being there. If the others are still sitting on the fence, your commitment will eventually bring them round.

9 ████████████████████████████████████

It's a great party. Everything is as it should be.

6 ███████████████   ███████████████

Alone in a crowd? Feeling like the odd one out? Hang in there. Wait for a sympathetic soul to show. Help is on the way.

6 ███████████████   ███████████████

Follow the feeling. There are unexpected good times to be had here. Remember to bring something to the party.

6 ███████████████   ███████████████

At first you're not so sure about this gathering. When you connect with a friend, there is laughter. Now you're glad you came.

≣≣ 46

Growing for It

the BOOK

SAYS :: *"The passion you have for the things you do enables you to push upward and reach for the stars."*

SEES :: you like a tree
drawing strength
from your roots
irresistibly growing
toward the light

SUGGESTS :: self-confidence makes all the difference
the tree of your life
is rooted in good earth
full of nutrients and moisture
your branches are supple and strong
the leaves know what to do with sunlight
so grow for it
make the effort to reach upward
and attain your goals
the incredible beauty of this tree:
it just goes on growing

and the CHANGING LINES ARE ::

6 ▬▬▬▬▬▬ ▬▬▬▬▬▬

6th

Progress for its own sake is not necessarily taking you where you want to go. Blindly pushing onward without a clear direction may well lead to exhaustion.

6 ▬▬▬▬▬▬ ▬▬▬▬▬▬

5th

Even the most successful people have to walk the walk. Keep your focus. Onward and upward—one step at a time.

6 ▬▬▬▬▬▬ ▬▬▬▬▬▬

4th

You're on. You're up!

9 ▬▬▬▬▬▬▬▬▬▬▬▬▬

3rd

When the timing is right, growth is easy. Success breeds success.

9 ▬▬▬▬▬▬▬▬▬▬▬▬▬

2nd

A humble offering made with sincerity has more value than the most lavish gift offered with none. It *is* the thought that counts.

6 ▬▬▬▬▬▬ ▬▬▬▬▬▬

1st

Vigorously pushing onward and upward with confidence is a winning combination.

47

Exhausting

the BOOK

SAYS :: *"When your best efforts are thwarted and your counsel rejected, it's easy to be demoralized. Get some rest and return to the fray when you are refreshed."*

SEES :: you like a dried-up lake
your resources depleted
your energy exhausted
in need of replenishment

SUGGESTS :: events seem to conspire against you
obstacles and setbacks confront you
people try to undermine you
but don't give up
if you can greet adversity with a smile
you will gain respect
if you can draw strength from distress
you will be revitalized
try to get a good night's sleep
things will look better in the morning

and the CHANGING LINES ARE ::

6 � ▰▰▰▰▰▰ ▰▰▰▰▰▰

You're still feeling shaky and uncertain about making your next move, still hurting from the last time it all went wrong. But things change. Let go of the past, hold on to the present, and move on.

9 ▰▰▰▰▰▰▰▰▰▰▰▰

You're not getting the help you need from the people out there who are supposed to be on your side. All you can do is quietly persevere, deriving strength from turning within to your God. Slowly but surely, joy returns.

9 ▰▰▰▰▰▰▰▰▰▰▰▰

You're caught up in an affluent society where you find the atmosphere oppressive. Embarrassment leads to withdrawal. Returning to your simpler way of life is a relief.

6 ▰▰▰▰▰▰ ▰▰▰▰▰▰

You bang your head against the wall and blame the wall for your head hurting. You lean on things that cannot support you, and you're surprised when you take a tumble.

9 ▰▰▰▰▰▰▰▰▰▰▰▰

Hang in there. Help is on the way. When you feel things getting on top of you, work is the worship in which your prayers for release are answered.

6 ▰▰▰▰▰▰ ▰▰▰▰▰▰

There are times when you are really up against it. Don't give in to the urge to be melancholy or depressed. You are a warrior, and the warrior must fight the good fight.

48

The Well

the BOOK

SAYS :: *"As a wellspring of kindness, you play*
a special role in your community.
But only if you keep the water pure."

SEES :: you like a well of pure water
a valuable resource
inevitably attracting
the thirsty to come and drink

SUGGESTS :: fashions come and go
societies change
economies fluctuate
but the need for water remains the same
just as people gather round a well
a kind person always attracts supporters
but the well must be kept in good order
if the community is going to benefit
preserve the integrity of your well
share the wealth within
you can afford to be kind
water is kindness

and the CHANGING LINES ARE ::

TOSS

6 ▬▬▬▬▬▬▬▬▬ ▬▬▬▬▬▬▬▬▬

6th

The well has an inexhaustible supply of pure water. There's plenty for all and everyone is welcome. The more people draw on your experience, the more you are replenished.

9 ▬▬▬▬▬▬▬▬▬▬▬▬▬▬▬▬▬▬▬▬▬▬

5th

Clear, cold water bubbles up from a spring within. You are inspired. People who come and drink from your well are truly refreshed.

6 ▬▬▬▬▬▬▬▬ ▬▬▬▬▬▬▬▬▬

4th

It's time to repair the well. The long-term advantage out-weighs the short-term inconvenience.

9 ▬▬▬▬▬▬▬▬▬▬▬▬▬▬▬▬▬▬▬▬▬▬

3rd

The well is fine, full of pure water, but nobody seems to know it's there. It would be good to let people know.

9 ▬▬▬▬▬▬▬▬▬▬▬▬▬▬▬▬▬▬▬▬▬▬

2nd

The well is fit only for fish and the bucket is broken. No wonder nobody comes to drink from your well.

6 ▬▬▬▬▬▬▬▬ ▬▬▬▬▬▬▬▬▬

1st

Nobody wants to drink from a muddy well. If your water is dirty, who will come and drink?

49
Welcoming Change

the BOOK

SAYS :: *"Change is good. By recognizing and*
acknowledging the cyclical nature of
life, by going with the flow, you can
enjoy success."

SEES :: you like a fire in the lake
talk about a revolution
as the seasons turn
comes a time of radical changes

SUGGESTS :: change is inevitable
summer yields to autumn
winter dissolves into spring
an animal molts
a snake sheds its skin
a spider renews its skeleton
you too are bound to change
it's all in the timing
when the time is right
you can change your world
when people believe in you
it really is your day

and the CHANGING LINES ARE :: **TOSS**

6 6th

Don't give up, no matter what. Once you've set your changes in motion, persevere. It's your initiative. You can't expect others, especially those with less at stake, to take it as seriously as you do.

9 5th

You're like a tiger, burning bright. The cause is just, and you make it clear why people should lend their support.

9 4th

When your own doubts disappear, people start to believe in you again. Now you can set about establishing a better way of doing things.

9 3rd

In times of great changes, take extra care. Try, try, and try again. Three is the magic number.

6 2nd

It's your day, your revolution. Be aware of what is likely to happen as a result of the changes you intend to make. Get ready for the consequences of your actions.

9 1st

Before you embark on any major changes, stop. Take a good look before you leap into the unknown.

50

The Cauldron

the BOOK

SAYS :: *"Now you're cooking! Like a ceremonial vessel that serves to nourish the people, you play a central role in the tribe."*

SEES :: you like a cauldron
full of nourishment
you're not too high
you're not too low
your position is perfect for you

SUGGESTS :: contemplate the cauldron
the cooking vessel at the heart
of ancient Chinese society
an object of great beauty
serving the practical purpose of cooking
while standing as a symbol
a sacred vessel in which to offer
the fruits of your labors to the gods
what you offer to the people of the world
with sincerity and reverence
will bring you good fortune and success

9

6th

The cauldron has rings of jade. Jade represents something truly precious. You are blessed. When fortune smiles on you, smile back.

6

5th

The cauldron has handles of gold. Working with it is a privilege and a pleasure that you can really feel. Lucky you.

9

4th

Confucius said, "Weak character coupled with honored place, little knowledge with big plans, limited powers with heavy responsibility, will seldom escape disaster."

9

3rd

Don't take this the wrong way, but something seems wrong with your handles. If people have difficulty grasping your cauldron, you defeat your own purpose. Turn this lack of recognition around: make it easy for people to get hold of you.

9

2nd

Your cauldron is filled with delicious food. This may make some people envious, but it doesn't bother you. You're enjoying the nourishment and happy to share. You have plenty.

6

1st

Turn that cauldron upside down. When the stew has turned or the soup is spoiled, get rid of it. Clean the cauldron thoroughly. Start fresh.

51
Rolling Thunder

the BOOK

SAYS :: *"Oh my God! Sometimes, a shock to the system will awaken you to the reality of your situation."*

SEES :: you being hit by a bolt from the blue
some kind of wake-up call
making you jump
though not necessarily for joy

SUGGESTS :: a major thunderstorm is awesome
in the true sense of the word
it awakens feelings of fear and wonder
of reverence and delight
if you can keep your composure
in the center of the storm
heightened perceptions
illuminate the state you are in
with such clarity
it can come as a shock
facing your problems brings relief
with relief comes laughter and jollity

and the CHANGING LINES ARE ::

6 ▬▬▬▬▬▬   ▬▬▬▬▬▬

When disaster strikes the person right next to you, it has a dramatic effect on you. A shock like this can provoke feelings of gratitude, making you realize how lucky you are.

6 ▬▬▬▬▬▬   ▬▬▬▬▬▬

The impact of the storm spreads far and wide. It's a dangerous situation. Stay calm, but be prepared for damages.

9 ▬▬▬▬▬▬▬▬▬▬▬▬▬▬

You're bogged down in a quagmire, the legacy of recent storms. You either get help or you have to be patient.

6 ▬▬▬▬▬▬   ▬▬▬▬▬▬

A shock to the system can be upsetting, but if it spurs you to take action, it's a good thing.

6 ▬▬▬▬▬▬   ▬▬▬▬▬▬

Wipe-out. You've been hit by a storm. The thing to do is accept your losses and start again. It will all come back to you.

9 ▬▬▬▬▬▬▬▬▬▬▬▬▬▬

One moment, you're in a state of shock. The next, you are laughing yourself silly. Now you can relax.

52

Keeping Still

the BOOK

SAYS :: *"Take some time: Forget your anxiety about the future, let go of your anguish about the past, focus on the moment called now."*

SEES :: you like a sacred mountain
serene
rising above the conflicts
the confusions of your world
solid as a rock

SUGGESTS :: your restless heart
needs to be still
for you to feel tranquil
safe at home
far from the madding crowd
find a peaceful spot
keeping the spine straight
breathe
as the conflicting opinions in your head
begin to subside
your clarity will arise
the sacred mountain within

and the CHANGING LINES ARE ::

9 ████████████████████████████████ 6th

You have achieved stillness. You feel much better. By keeping
still and trusting your own feelings, you find the solutions, not
just for your immediate situation but for your whole life. The
power of keeping still is mighty indeed. Peace. Good fortune.

6 ██████████████   ██████████████ 5th

Keep your own counsel. As the confusing and conflicting
opinions of other people die down, you find your answers.
You know what to do.

6 ██████████████   ██████████████ 4th

Keep the torso still and the spine in line. The heart can start
to heal.

9 ████████████████████████████████ 3rd

Try not to try too hard. Drop the shoulders. When you can
relax into your meditation, a natural feeling of calm will
arise.

6 ██████████████   ██████████████ 2nd

You are swept along by strong currents. If you resist, your
limbs are going to ache.

6 ██████████████   ██████████████ 1st

Begin with the toes and work your way up. Simply by keeping still, you can get back in touch with your inner sense.

53

Tree of Life

the BOOK

SAYS :: *"Take a step back and look at the big picture. How you have grown, and how much you still have to grow!"*

SEES :: you like a tree on a hill
slowly developing roots
surely spreading branches
you stand tall and dignified
an example to us all

SUGGESTS :: you
take your time
let nature do the work
look: how kind is the tree
it spreads its branches as shade
provides shelter and nourishment
gives freely of its bounty
remains true to its nature
in every season
so calm
so right
so you
letting nature take its course brings success

and the CHANGING LINES ARE ::

9

Your progress is complete. You have attained your goal. It's a time for celebration. More than a festive occasion, this is an affirmation of the circle of life and your place in it. What a beautiful dance it is.

9

Your progress has taken you to an elevated position. It's easy to become isolated and misunderstood. Don't let it get to you. You will be vindicated in the end.

6

As you progress toward your distant goal, there will come times of danger and uncertainty. Even if it's only temporary, a safe place to land is a blessing. Make the most of it.

9

Gradual progress in the right direction is infinitely preferable to huge strides in the wrong direction. Slowly but surely, find the way that will take you where you want to go, and stick to it.

6

You're making good progress and have completed the first stage. A little celebration is in order.

6

If you're starting something new, you can expect to get some resistance. But don't give up. You are definitely making progress.

54

Falling for Love

the BOOK

SAYS :: *"Every day is a miracle waiting to happen, and falling in love means being free."*

SEES :: you like a storm over a lake
the water stirred up
your equanimity disturbed
by unusual emotions

SUGGESTS :: life is full of surprises
like when you fall in love
with a person or a place
with a song or an idea
with a story or a prayer
defenses come down
your heart leaps within you
the tyranny of time is overthrown
all of a sudden, nothing's a chore!
losing yourself in the other
you let yourself go
only to discover:
the ones you love the most
drive you the craziest

and the CHANGING LINES ARE ::

TOSS

6 ▬▬▬▬▬ ▬▬▬▬▬ 6th

Are you just going through the motions? If you're not feeling it, why are you doing it?

6 ▬▬▬▬▬ ▬▬▬▬▬ 5th

The moon that is nearly full is an exquisite sight. Natural modesty combined with great beauty is an irresistible combination.

9 ▬▬▬▬▬▬▬▬▬▬ 4th

Give your love space to grow. Allow it time to blossom.

6 ▬▬▬▬▬ ▬▬▬▬▬ 3rd

Are you a slave of your desires? Are you a victim of your passions? If the answer is yes, you're asking for trouble and you'll probably get it.

9 ▬▬▬▬▬▬▬▬▬▬ 2nd

In the country of the blind, the one-eyed man is king. In any relationship, the one who can see clearly will be the one who calls the shots.

9 ▬▬▬▬▬▬▬▬▬▬ 1st

You've been crippled by relationships in the past. Now, with this new love, you find you can walk again.

55

A Time of Abundance

the BOOK

SAYS :: *"It's time for you to share your wealth with the world and, in turn, reap your rewards."*

SEES :: the sun at midday
you
at the peak of your powers
radiating pure energy
creating abundance

SUGGESTS :: the zenith of the sun's progress
is a fleeting moment in time
the abundance of summer cannot last
but don't be sad
sadness doesn't suit you
make the most of this time
rejoice in your good fortune
share your wealth with the world
and the world will share its wealth with you

and the CHANGING LINES ARE ::

6 ▬▬▬▬▬▬   ▬▬▬▬▬▬   6th

You're getting what you want. But if you alienate family and friends in the process, you could end up feeling isolated.

6 ▬▬▬▬▬▬   ▬▬▬▬▬▬   5th

You know what to do—the way is clear. Your good fortune awaits you.

9 ▬▬▬▬▬▬▬▬▬▬▬▬▬▬▬   4th

The eclipse is passing. The light is returning. Friends and allies are at hand. Be glad the livelong day.

9 ▬▬▬▬▬▬▬▬▬▬▬▬▬▬▬   3rd

Your brilliance is being obscured by your detractors. There's not a lot you can do about it for now. But it's bound to change.

6 ▬▬▬▬▬▬   ▬▬▬▬▬▬   2nd

Are you being eclipsed? Don't let it get to you. The nature of an eclipse is that it's short lived. You are going to shine again.

9 ▬▬▬▬▬▬▬▬▬▬▬▬▬▬▬   1st

Sometimes two heads *are* better than one.

56

The Wanderer

the BOOK

SAYS :: *"Good fortune awaits the traveler who honors the law of the road: Gratitude is the attitude."*

SEES :: a fire on the mountain
a light to guide you
on your travels
a beacon to give you hope

SUGGESTS :: when you're a stranger in a strange land
a pleasant manner
a willingness to engage
the innocence of a child
will open many doors for you
stay with good people
and your journey will go well
do all you can
to protect your state of mind
because life is not without its hazards

and the CHANGING LINES ARE ::

TOSS

9

6th

Don't get so carried away with your wanderings that you put your home at risk. A bird without a nest may well have cause to lament.

6

5th

If you know how to play the game and can impress the locals with your ability, you can win friends and influence. The adventurer will often reap rich rewards away from home.

9

4th

You find shelter from the storm. But it doesn't mean you can lower your guard. You're still a stranger.

9

3rd

When a stranger in a strange land has no dependable friends or sympathetic contacts, the situation becomes dangerous. Take care out there.

6

2nd

An inn at the crossroads. You find a helper and friend. Lucky.

6

1st

The first rule of the road: Keep your cool. Don't play the fool. When people know you better, you can do your comedy routine. Maybe.

57

Breezing Along

the BOOK

SAYS :: *"You penetrate every aspect of the situation, making sure things keep moving in the right direction."*

SEES :: you like a summer breeze
clearing your sky of clouds
revealing the serenity of the sky

SUGGESTS :: be like the wind
that keeps blowing in the same direction
you don't bluster about
constantly changing your approach
you are consistent in your aims
always moving toward your goal
you communicate your purpose clearly
consistently
the effects are subtle yet irresistible
you just keep coming

and the **CHANGING LINES ARE** ::

TOSS

9 ██

6th

Your investigations into the darker corners of your world have gone far enough. You put yourself at risk if you continue to probe. Come back to the light.

9 ██

5th

As your plan unfolds, monitor your progress. Evaluate the results. Such painstaking work will increase your chances of a long-term success.

6 ████████████████   ████████████████

4th

Your hunt is a great success. Three's a charm.

9 ██

3rd

You've contemplated this question enough already. If you don't act decisively soon, you'll just be assailed by fresh doubts.

9 ██

2nd

Are there skeletons in your closet? Monsters under your bed? When you stir up ghosts, some sort of exorcism may be required.

6 ████████████████   ████████████████

1st

Drifting back and forth, a victim of indecision, will expose you to danger. No doubt about it: Decisive action is the order of the day.

58

The Joyful Lake

the BOOK

SAYS :: *"Joy upon joy! The happiness you feel allows you to be gentle and kind to those around you."*

SEES :: two lakes
feeding into each other
people pooling their knowledge
in a friendly environment
where learning is fun

SUGGESTS :: dive in
creating delightful patterns
reflections of the joy you feel inside
finding yourself in this beautiful place
you feel free to express yourself
your appreciation is shared by others
together you discover ways
to reflect the water's love of the sky

6 ▬▬▬▬▬▬▬   ▬▬▬▬▬▬▬   6th

There is the joy that springs from within. Indulge in it as much as you like. But be wary of the enjoyments that come from outside. Wanton indulgence in such pleasures will put you at risk.

9 ▬▬▬▬▬▬▬▬▬▬▬▬▬▬▬   5th

When you're enjoying yourself, your guard is down. Dangerous forces may be lurking. A little security is advisable.

9 ▬▬▬▬▬▬▬▬▬▬▬▬▬▬▬   4th

Chasing after pleasure all too often ends in pain. The day you realize this is a good day.

6 ▬▬▬▬▬▬▬   ▬▬▬▬▬▬▬   3rd

Yes, you can have too much of a good thing. Overindulgence leads to grief.

9 ▬▬▬▬▬▬▬▬▬▬▬▬▬▬▬   2nd

This joy is within you. You contain it. They can't take it away from you even if they try.

9 ▬▬▬▬▬▬▬▬▬▬▬▬▬▬▬   1st

A contented heart. Pure joy. When you feel blessed, you are blessed.

59
Dissolving

the BOOK

SAYS :: *"When pride and ego create barriers between people, your love can dissolve them—like ice melting in the sun."*

SEES :: you like the warm winds of spring
melting the ice of winter
releasing liquid happiness
back into your world

SUGGESTS :: create a sanctuary
where love holds sway
in the gentle warmth of devotion
the hard edges dissolve
through ceremony and celebration
feelings of awe awaken
when the music plays
the spirit dances
fellowship is restored
your intuitions fulfilled
you can end your winter of discontent
simply by embracing the content of spring

and the CHANGING LINES ARE ::

9 ██████████████████████████████

You can't always fulfill the expectations of others, especially family members. Sometimes you have to do your own thing.

9 ██████████████████████████████

You are the one to bring about the recovery. Your solution is just what is needed. Shout it out if you have to, but let the people know.

6 ████████████   ████████████

Don't follow the crowd. Dare to be different. When you work hard to make your unique contribution, it will be appreciated.

6 ████████████   ████████████

Get over yourself. Dive into the work. The harder you work, the better you feel.

9 ██████████████████████████████

Feeling alienated? Are people getting you down? Hurry back to where you belong. Stay there until you feel yourself again.

6 ████████████   ████████████

Nip it in the bud. When misunderstandings threaten the harmony of the group, stop them before they start.

60
Knowing Your Limitations

the BOOK

SAYS :: *"With no boundaries, the lake would be a swamp; without its banks, the river could not flow."*

SEES :: you like a body of water
clearly defined
self-contained
content with your lot

SUGGESTS :: establish your boundaries
set limits
work out a budget and stick to it
make a line in the sand
and do not cross this line
by rising to the little challenges
of living simply
you can enjoy the enormous satisfaction
of simply living

and the CHANGING LINES ARE ::

6 ▬▬▬▬▬▬▬▬   ▬▬▬▬▬▬▬▬   6th

Don't be so stingy with yourself. Set limits on the limits. You know what they say: Moderation in all things, including moderation.

9 ▬▬▬▬▬▬▬▬▬▬▬▬▬▬▬▬▬▬▬   5th

Accepting limitations graciously makes life sweet. Where you lead, others will follow.

6 ▬▬▬▬▬▬▬▬   ▬▬▬▬▬▬▬▬   4th

Like the banks of a river, limitations help direct you. Accept them. Be content. Go with the flow.

6 ▬▬▬▬▬▬▬▬   ▬▬▬▬▬▬▬▬   3rd

If you go on self-indulging, you'll be sorry. If you go on over-indulging, you'll be *very* sorry.

9 ▬▬▬▬▬▬▬▬▬▬▬▬▬▬▬▬▬▬▬   2nd

Time to get out more. Let your light shine. It could be an illuminating experience for everyone, including you.

9 ▬▬▬▬▬▬▬▬▬▬▬▬▬▬▬▬▬▬▬   1st

Don't expose yourself to unnecessary risks. In dangerous times, keeping a low profile is your safest strategy.

61

Inner Truth

the BOOK

SAYS :: *"Free yourself from prejudice so that*
your actions can be based on what
you know to be true."

SEES :: a gentle wind blowing
the surface of the water
making the invisible visible
inciting waves of joy

SUGGESTS :: hold on to your inner truth
sometimes a good idea is an egg
it needs warmth and protection
it will come to life
when the time is right
when dealing with difficult people
use your intuitive ability
to discover what will appeal to them
about the truth you're trying to get across
when you stop judging so much
and start understanding a little more
you can bring out the best
in everyone—including yourself

and the CHANGING LINES ARE ::

9

The rooster crows at the break of day. It may make a good alarm call, but you need more than crowing to get you through the day.

9

Your inner truth is the foundation of your relationships in the world. When you are true to yourself, you create a circle of strength around you.

6

As the moon derives its radiance from the sun, your inner truth is intensified by the love and respect you feel for the teacher who inspires you.

6

You're riding a roller coaster of emotions. One moment you're on top of the world, the next you're in the abyss. All the fun of the affair!

9

Express your real feelings, sincerely and clearly, and your circle of influence will grow.

9

The more you depend on the truth of others, the weaker you become. Tap into what's true for you. When you get in touch with your own truth, anxiety goes away.

62

Keeping Your Feet on the Ground

the BOOK

SAYS :: *"Come back to earth. Don't try to fly so high. Not now. If your high-flying stunts result in the loss of your nest, you'll be sorry."*

SEES :: you like attending to the details
to make the big picture
a true work of art
a bird in flight tells you
think small—think beautiful

SUGGESTS :: by achieving tiny victories
you are working toward
something truly magnificent
so play your part as well as you can
for you to succeed
in so ambitious a task
you'd better be extremely conscientious
only the lowly know
how wonderful it is to be uplifted
little things make a big difference

and the CHANGING LINES ARE ::

6 ▆▆▆▆▆▆▆▆▆   ▆▆▆▆▆▆▆▆▆

6th

There's a time to fly high and a time to stay close to the ground. Attend to the little things. God is in the details.

6 ▆▆▆▆▆▆▆▆▆   ▆▆▆▆▆▆▆▆▆

5th

High clouds, no rain. You need the support of good people you can trust to help you through the dry spell.

9 ▆▆▆▆▆▆▆▆▆▆▆▆▆▆▆▆▆▆▆▆

4th

Caution is called for. If you try to force your way now, you're likely to cause more damage. Patience. Your day will come.

9 ▆▆▆▆▆▆▆▆▆▆▆▆▆▆▆▆▆▆▆▆

3rd

If you're not careful, someone is liable to sneak up on you and attack. Pay attention!

6 ▆▆▆▆▆▆▆▆▆   ▆▆▆▆▆▆▆▆▆

2nd

Go through the appropriate channels. Sometimes you just cannot beat the system.

6 ▆▆▆▆▆▆▆▆▆   ▆▆▆▆▆▆▆▆▆

1st

What happens if a fledgling tries to fly before it's ready?

63

Establishing the New

the BOOK

SAYS :: *"When everything has gone your way and you've got what you wanted, it's time to be extra careful."*

SEES :: a kettle boiling above a fire
caution is required
because if the water boils over
it will extinguish the flames
no tea for two

SUGGESTS :: things are coming together
your house is set in order
you are achieving your goals
when everything's going so well
complacency can take over
and your new order reverts to chaos
you'd be wise to foresee the dangers
and difficulties to come
when you can see it coming
you can stop it before it starts

and the CHANGING LINES ARE ::

6 ████████████████   ████████████████

Tough times. The less you look back and the more you move forward, the more likely you are to get into a better place.

9 ██

In the rush of events surrounding the new order, extravagant gestures are being made on every side. But your humble offering, made with sincerity, will have a more lasting influence.

6 ██████████████   ████████████████

The finest clothes will one day turn to rags. Even the most stylish wardrobe needs refreshing.

9 ██

After completion, a clear policy is essential, especially when the new order is threatened by greedy people.

6 ████████████████   ████████████████

Wait for it! When the new order is established and the honors are being handed out, don't worry if you are overlooked. Your worth will be recognized and rewarded if you can be patient.

9 ██

Don't get carried away. Success is intoxicating, but you should rein in that unbridled enthusiasm of yours or you might fall flat on your face.

64
Before Completing

the BOOK

SAYS :: *"You're on the cusp between the old order and the new. Take as much care with the last step of the journey as with the first."*

SEES :: you like a fire on the water
opposing elements
somehow joined
yet kept separate

SUGGESTS :: tread carefully like an old fox
crossing a frozen river
alert to the slightest crack
in a time of transition
the priority has to be making it
safely to the other side
as fire leaps up
reaching for the sun
as water flows down
drawn to the ocean
you will find your true home
in the end
(and see it for the first time)

and the CHANGING LINES ARE ::

9 ████████████████████████████████████

Congratulations! Time to celebrate. But don't overdo it. The new era is about to begin, and you'll appreciate it more with a clear head. In the end, it's time to start again.

6 ████████████   ████████████

You have succeeded. Your time has come. Like sunshine after rain, like new growth in the forest after a fire, the new era is beautiful and full of joy.

9 ████████████████████████████████████

Be bold and decisive. Persevere. The time for doubt and hesitation is over. Ring out the old, bring on the new.

6 ████████████   ████████████

A time of transition can expose you to threats and dangers you don't normally have to deal with. Helping hands may well be required to get you safely across to the other side.

9 ████████████████████████████████████

S-T-O-P: Stop, Think, Organize, Proceed.

6 ████████████   ████████████

Discretion is the better part of valor, especially during a time of transition. Picture an inexperienced fox running onto thin ice.

III.

OUTRO

WHAT IS an ORACLE?

"The I Ching is an oracle: something that speaks. Talking with an oracle is called divination. When you divine, you listen attentively to hear the question you are asking and the oracle's answer. . . . In a world that seems noisier than ever, divination offers a quiet refuge for listening. It is the place where your inner guidance comes into resonance with present truth."

—HILARY BARRETT, *I Ching: Walking Your Path, Creating Your Future*

The most famous oracle in the history of Western civilization was the Temple of Apollo at Delphi in Greece. For nearly a thousand years, the Delphic oracle was the spiritual center of the mighty Greek empire. Everyone from kings and queens to ordinary everyday people would make the pilgrimage to Delphi to find answers to all sorts of questions.

In China, *The Book of Changes* was equally renowned as an oracle. The Chinese people have consulted it for guidance or prophecy for millennia. It has been long revered as an authoritative, wise, and insightful adviser. Now you, too, can consult it to gain perspective on your life and answers to your questions.

How it works is a mystery. For example, when I used the three-coin method to ask *The Book* the question, "What is an oracle?" it told me: "By finding a high place, you gain the perspective you need."

Now, this is the very thing about *The Book of Changes* that impressed Carl Jung so profoundly when he consulted it, as he expressed in the foreword to the classic 1950 edition: How can something so illogical make so much sense?

Since time immemorial, people have looked for a deeper meaning and a higher purpose in this life. The oracle, embodied in the *I Ching*, provides you many clues as to how to find both.

There was a famous saying over the entrance to the sanctuary surrounding the oracle at Delphi: "Know thyself." *The Little Book of Changes* offers you a way to do just that.

WHAT'S in a HEXAGRAM?

Each hexagram is composed of two three-line figures called trigrams, an upper and a lower—also called the outer and inner. The trigrams are made up of unbroken (yang) lines and broken (yin) lines. If you look at the chart on page 13, you can see there are eight trigrams. Each one is a symbol derived from nature. Originally, these trigrams were all the sages of ancient China needed for divination. Later, combining them in pairs yielded the 64 (8 x 8) hexagrams we have today.

≡ **Ch'ien = Heaven.** Heaven represents the Creative. All three lines are yang, and yang is associated with the masculine, the sky, and forcefulness. Full of energy and strength, this trigram indicates the ability to make things happen.

≡≡ **K'un = Earth.** Earth represents the Receptive. All three lines are yin, and yin is associated with the feminine, the earth, and nurturing. Full of love and compassion, this trigram indicates the ability to let it be.

≡≡ **Chên = Thunder.** Thunder represents the Arousing. It can be a shock like a thunderclap exploding directly overhead or a bolt of lightning cracking open the sky. It is awesome. This trigram is associated with movement, excitement, and dramatic changes.

☰☰ **Sun = Wind.** Wind represents the Gentle. The wind is the least predictable component of a weather system. A shape-shifter, it can gently penetrate any situation. This trigram is associated with flexibility, subtlety, and being able to adapt to changing circumstances.

☰☰ **Tuì = Lake.** Lake represents the Joyful. This is a beautiful scene where people can commune with nature and each other. It's like a pool of shared wisdom. This trigram is associated with celebrating, expressing yourself, and pleasure.

☰☰ **Kên = Mountain.** Mountain represents Keeping Still. All over the world, the mountain has been traditionally considered a sacred site, a place to retreat in silence. This trigram is associated with stillness, serenity, and gaining perspective.

☰☰ **K'an = Water.** Water represents the Abysmal. While water is a source of life and teaches us the lesson of flowing, deep waters hold many hazards. Beware. This trigram is associated with hardship, dangerous journeys, and remaining true to your nature.

☰☰ **Li = Fire.** Fire represents the Clinging. Like water, fire is an element that delivers great benefits yet can also bring great harm. Flames depend on fuel to keep burning. This trigram is associated with light-giving, warmth, and clarity.

A BRIEF HISTORY of the BOOK

The original *I Ching* or *Book of Changes* was composed so long ago, we really don't know that much about it. I could tell you that its authorship has been attributed to Fu Hsi, King Wen, and the Duke of Zhou. But unless you're a student of Chinese history, this won't mean a thing.

We do know that *The Book* had an enormous influence over Chinese culture for thousands of years. As Edward L. Shaughnessy says in *The Classic of Changes*, "Virtually every major figure in China's intellectual tradition has had something to say about the text. The enigmatic images of its hexagram and line statements have been adapted to every life situation, while the world view of its commentary is arguably the most sophisticated statement of the thought that has been so fundamental to all of China's philosophical systems."

> *The very first time I did this, I was overawed to a degree that amounted to fright, so strong was the impression of having received an answer to my question from a living, breathing person. . . . The astonishing effect emphasize[s] how extraordinarily accurate and . . . personal are its answers.*
>
> —JOHN BLOFELD, *I Ching: The Book of Change*

The Confucian Connection

The first translation of the *I Ching* into English was the work of the missionary and Chinese scholar James Legge in 1882. In his preface, we find the tradition that connects *The Book* with Confucius: "Confucius is reported to have said on one occasion, 'If some years were added to my life, I would give fifty to the study of the *I Ching*, and might then escape falling into great errors.'" Sze-mâ Khien, the first great Chinese historian, who died in about 85 BC, stated that, in the closing years of his life, Confucius became fond of the *I Ching* and wrote various appendixes to it; that he read his copy of it so much that the leathern thongs (by which the tablets containing it were bound together) were thrice worn out; and that he had said, "Give me several years more, and I should be master of the *I Ching*."

Now, we'll never know if this is true or not. We do know that the followers of Confucius ascribed much of the content of *The Book* to their great teacher and that these ideas have been a huge influence over Chinese thought and culture.

We also know that, in 1973, archaeologists investigating a tomb in Mawangdui in China discovered more than twenty texts written on silk, including the earliest known copy of the *I Ching*. That evidence suggests it was written around 200 BC, about three centuries *after* Confucius lived. Whoever the original authors were, one thing's for sure: *The Book of Changes* is a very old book indeed—yet its content is surprisingly relevant to our age.

Many Visions, Many Versions

There is no shortage of interpretations of *The Book of Changes*, and still they keep coming. There are Taoist, Buddhist, biblical, feminist, astrological, numerological, pantheistic, and psychological versions. They range from super-simple to stupendously complex. Some are as lucid as the sky with diamonds; others are as clear as mud. The mere fact that so many versions of this ancient book have been written is a testament to its unique character and unusual properties. It appears to work like a magic mirror in which people of all cultures and creeds see their own beliefs reflected and their worldview endorsed. *The Book* is old enough, wise enough, and big enough to accept all these perceptions and projections with equanimity.

Open up your favorite search engine and enter *"I Ching"* and/or *"Book of Changes,"* and you can see for yourself how many interpretations are out there. Please feel free to explore as many as you like. But for me, there is one I would wholeheartedly recommend: the classic 1950 edition, published by the Bollingen Foundation. It was translated from Chinese into German by Richard Wilhelm and then beautifully rendered into English by Cary F. Baynes.

Now, unlike Confucius, I haven't worn out the bindings on this remarkable book, but it has been my companion for many years. I come back to it over and over again, like an animal that has been traveling across the

> The Book of Changes—I Ching *in Chinese*—is unquestionably one of the most important books in the world's literature. Nearly all that is greatest and most significant in the three thousand years of Chinese cultural history has either taken its inspiration from this book, or has exerted an influence on the interpretation of its text. Therefore, it may safely be said that the seasoned wisdom of thousands of years has gone into the making of the I Ching.
>
> —RICHARD WILHELM

desert returns to its favorite oasis. The water is pure, the well is deep, the surroundings are elegant and cultured. Like a beautiful garden that goes on revealing fresh delights according to the time of day and the changing of the seasons, the Wilhelm version continues to fascinate and inspire, offering me profound reflections, insights, and revelations.

Joy in Pure Wisdom

Richard Wilhelm was a true pioneer. He left his home in Germany in 1899 and traveled to China as a Christian missionary. But rather than converting the Chinese, he discovered the sacred books of China and a spiritual legacy that transformed his belief system. With a natural linguistic ability and a powerful rapport with his subject matter, he studied the classics. Then, in 1911, he met the sage who was to become his "honoured teacher."

Lao Nai-hsuan was one of many eminent scholars Wilhelm encountered while living in Tsingtao, and Mr.

> " *Your chosen question starts your conversation with the oracle and it defines what you will hear in the response. . . . The help you can receive from a reading depends strongly on your question. The clearer you are about what you're asking, the easier you'll find it to understand and connect with the response. And the more conscious and intentional your question— the more clearly you know why you are asking it—the easier it is to integrate and use the answer.* "

—Hilary Barrett, *I Ching: Walking Your Path, Creating Your Future*

Lao introduced him to *The Book of Changes*. This was a life-changing experience for the young German that he describes in the preface to his translation: "Under his experienced guidance I wandered entranced through this strange yet familiar world. Our translation of the text was made after detailed discussion. Those were rare hours of inspiration that I spent with my aged master."

Their collaboration was interrupted by the advent of World War I, and they were separated for some years. Then Mr. Lao returned after the war to Tsingtao, and they resumed work on their translation. It wasn't until 1923 that Wilhelm considered the book complete: "In the warm days of a Peking summer the work was finally brought to conclusion. Recast again and again, the text has at last attained a form that—though it falls far short of my wish—makes it possible for me to give the book to the world. May the same joy in pure wisdom be the part of those who read the translation as was mine while I worked upon it."

Introducing the Book to the West
Even though Legge's translation dates back to 1882 and an edition of Wilhelm's translation was published in 1923 in Germany, it took another twenty-seven years for *The Book of Changes* to be properly introduced to the English-speaking world. This was largely due to the efforts of one man, the famous psychologist and student of all things esoteric, Carl Jung. Jung was deeply impressed both by

the man and by his translation of the *I Ching*. Even though Wilhelm died in 1930 from the amoebic dysentery he had contracted in China, Jung had always wanted to bring his work to a wider audience. Finally, in 1950, the Wilhelm translation was published by the Bollingen Foundation with a foreword by Jung.

This foreword still stands as a brilliant introduction to *The Book of Changes*. It begins: "Since I am not a sinologue [*a scholar of classical Chinese language and literature*], a foreword from my hand must be a testimonial of my individual experience with this great and singular book." Jung goes on to present a characteristically intelligent and original approach to explaining the profound differences between the European and Chinese mindsets. Then he conducts a simple but bold experiment: He asks *The Book of Changes* "strictly in accordance with the Chinese conception, asking its judgment about its present situation, i.e., my intention to present it to the Western mind."

Jung muses, "Why not venture a dialogue with an ancient book that purports to be animated [*endowed with the qualities of life*]? There can be no harm in it, and the reader may watch a psychological procedure that has been carried out throughout the millennia of Chinese civilization, representing to a Confucius or a Lao-tse both a supreme expression of spiritual authority and a philosophical enigma. I made use of the coin method and the answer obtained was [*using the present translation*]:

50

The Cauldron

the BOOK

SAYS :: *"Now you're cooking! Like*
a ceremonial vessel that serves
to nourish the people, you play
a central role in the tribe."

SEES :: you like a cauldron
full of nourishment
you're not too high
you're not too low
your position is perfect for you

SUGGESTS :: contemplate the cauldron
the cooking vessel at the heart
of ancient Chinese society
an object of great beauty
serving the practical purpose of cooking
while standing as a symbol
a sacred vessel in which to offer
the fruits of your labors to the gods
what you offer to the people of the world
with sincerity and reverence
will bring you good fortune and success

The way the coins landed gave Jung two changing lines, providing more detail to the first answer and leading him to a second reading.

2nd **9** ████████████████████████████████████

Your cauldron is filled with delicious food. This may make some people envious, but it doesn't bother you. You're enjoying the nourishment for yourself and happy to share. You have plenty.

3rd **9** ████████████████████████████████████

Don't take this the wrong way, but something seems wrong with your handles. If people have difficulty grasping your cauldron, you defeat your own purpose. Turn this lack of recognition around: make it easy for people to get hold of you.

Jung continues to muse: "The answer given in these two salient lines requires no particular subtlety of interpretation, no artifices, no unusual knowledge. Anyone with a little common sense can understand the meaning of the answer. But how has this reaction come about? Because I threw three small coins in the air and let them fall, roll, and come to rest, heads up or tails up, as the case may be. This odd fact that a reaction that makes sense arises out of a technique seemingly excluding all sense from the outset, is the great achievement of the *I Ching*. The instance I have just given is not unique; meaningful answers are the rule."

> *Any kind of question can be put to the I Ching for advice, comment and recommendations. . . . As an oracle the I Ching offers interpretations of great wisdom that will provide a guide at each moment in time and each stage in your life. It will help you to identify what will be significant turning points. . . . It can be regarded as a friend, there to cheer, comfort, and inspire you; or rather as an invisible friend—your higher self—given voice.*

—LILLIAN TOO, *The New I Ching*

As we showed you in the introduction, if you throw three heads or three tails, the line turns into its opposite. So in this case, Jung got three heads on the second and third throws. Turning these lines into their opposites led Jung to the second half of his answer: 35. Making Progress. Now, as I work on this new interpretation of the *I Ching* in the warm days of a Cornish summer, I can't help noticing that this is the same reading given to me when I asked the same question, over sixty years later.

As Jung himself concluded about the response he got from *The Book*: "It pleased and satisfied me."

FRIENDS from FAR AWAY

On the eighth hour of the eighth day of the eighth month of the eighth year of the new millennium, the 2008 Olympic Games kicked off in Beijing. As three billion people tuned in to watch one of the most spectacular displays of Chinese culture ever seen, whom did they choose to represent China to the world?

Around 2,500 years ago, a man walked the earth, gathering followers and teaching them his Way. His name was Kong Qiu, or, as he is more widely known, Confucius.

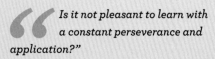

Is it not pleasant to learn with a constant perseverance and application?"

"Is it not delightful to have friends coming from distant quarters?"

"Is he not a man of complete virtue who feels no discomposure though men may take no note of him?"

—*THE ANALECTS OF CONFUCIUS*, translated by James Legge

And it was a quotation attributed to Confucius that went out to the billions watching in so many countries around the world: "When friends from far away come to visit—is it not a delight?"

I was watching the ceremony in my living room in England. I was blown away by the fact that the man who had such an influence in the ancient world still has such a presence in our modern one.

The quotation still resonates with me to this day on a deeper level. In a way, it describes how I feel when I consult *The Book of Changes*: that I am being visited by old friends, wise friends, good friends. "Friends from far away."

I'll leave you with a final word from Richard Wilhelm's son, Hellmut, in his preface to the third edition of his father's *I Ching*: "It is with delight and not without a certain pride that I see this translation of *The Book of Changes* presented in a new edition."

ACKNOWLEDGMENTS

RAOUL GOFF, founder and CEO of Mandala Publishing, for being open, wise, and hip to the potential of this little book.

RACHEL O'REILLY, for "getting" it straight away and making it happen.

JAKE GERLI, for guiding me through many drafts to this final form.

MARK BURSTEIN, for an excellent edit and polish.

DAGMAR TROJANEK, for her elegant response to the design challenges of such a book.

TO EVERYONE who has helped and encouraged me to complete this little book, my heartfelt thanks.

ABOUT the AUTHOR

Dreamer, poet, lyricist, mystic, musician, and writer, **PETER CRISP** was born in South Africa. He was transported as a baby by ship to England, where he grew up on a free-range farm in East Anglia. Since leaving home at the age of sixteen, he has spent half his adult life on the West Coast of America and half in the UK. He considers himself to be, like Thomas Paine, "a citizen of the world." Having consulted the *I Ching* for more than forty years, he is still frequently surprised by its magical properties.

Crisp currently resides on the dramatic Atlantic coast of North Cornwall, where he works under the banner of "Ghostwriter in the Sky." He is busy putting the finishing touches on *The Adventures of the Rainbow Gypsies* and *The Halcyon Days of Peter White*. These are true stories from the 1960s and early 1970s that are quite unbelievable. But "truth," as Lord Byron observed, "is always strange—stranger than fiction."

MANDALA
PUBLISHING

PO Box 3088
San Rafael, CA 94912
www.mandalapublishing.com

Copyright © 2012 Peter Crisp

Library of Congress Cataloging-in-Publication Data available.

ISBN: 978-1-60887-068-4

ROOTS of PEACE   REPLANTED PAPER

Insight Editions, in association with Roots of Peace, will plant two trees
for each tree used in the manufacturing of this book. Roots of Peace is
an internationally renowned humanitarian organization dedicated to
eradicating land mines worldwide and converting war-torn lands into
productive farms and wildlife habitats. Together, we will plant two million
fruit and nut trees in Afghanistan and provide farmers there with the
skills and support necessary for sustainable land use.

Manufactured in China

10 9 8 7 6 5 4 3 2 1

Designed by Dagmar Trojanek